A Cowboy's Life

A Cowboy's Life

Bob Lilly with Kristine Setting Clark

TRIUMPH
BOOKS

Library of Congress Cataloging-in-Publication Data

Lilly, Bob.
A Cowboy's life / Bob Lilly and Kristine Setting Clark.
   p. cm.
Includes bibliographical references.
ISBN-13: 978-1-60078-101-8
ISBN-10: 1-60078-101-2
1. Lilly, Bob. 2. Football players—United States—Biography. 3.
Dallas Cowboys (Football team)—History. I. Clark, Kristine Setting,
1950- II. Title.
GV939.L55 2008
796.332092—dc22
[B]   2008021691

This book is available in quantity at special discounts for your group or organization. For further information, contact:

Triumph Books
542 South Dearborn Street
Suite 750
Chicago, Illinois 60605
(312) 939-3330
Fax (312) 663-3557

Printed in U.S.A.
ISBN: 978-1-60078-101-8
Design by Sue Knopf

*This book is dedicated to
Coach Tom Landry.*

Contents

ix   **Foreword** by Roger Staubach

xiii **Acknowledgments**

xv   **Introduction** by Steve Sabol

First Quarter: The Early Years

3   **Chapter 1:** My Dad, My Hero

9   **Chapter 2:** The Letter

13   **Chapter 3:** Texas Christian University

Second Quarter: From Nobody's Team to America's Team

23   **Chapter 4:** A Cowboy First

29   **Chapter 5:** Coach Tom Landry: A Man for All Seasons

35   **Chapter 6:** The Birth of the Cowboys

41   **Chapter 7:** Putting the Team Together

47   **Chapter 8:** Stepping It Up

57   **Chapter 9:** Tragedy Strikes

61   **Chapter 10:** Improving the Team with Technology and the Flex

71   **Chapter 11:** Post-Merger Successes

75   **Chapter 12:** We Can Do Everything but Win the Big One

79   **Chapter 13:** Our Season to Shine Becomes a Season of Sadness

83   **Chapter 14:** Quarterback Controversy and Changes Afoot

89   **Chapter 15:** Duane Thomas Makes the Scene

99   **Chapter 16:** Winning the Big One

107 **Chapter 17:** Farewells

113 **Chapter 18:** Games I Will Never Forget

Third Quarter: Characters, Heroes, and Great Leading Men

131 **Chapter 19:** The Originals

147 **Chapter 20:** Players Year by Year

207 **Chapter 21:** The Coaching Staff

Fourth Quarter: Life after Football

217 **Chapter 22:** Battle Scars

227 **Chapter 23:** Postgridiron Employment

231 **Chapter 24:** The Ring of Honor and the Hall of Fame

241 **Chapter 25:** The Camera's Eye

245 **Appendix:** Stats, Accolades, Honors, and Achievements

247 **Sources**

Foreword

IT'S BEEN SAID THAT BOB LILLY WAS THE GREATEST defensive tackle to ever play the game. I am a testament to that statement.

After serving my military obligation with the United States Navy, I joined the Dallas Cowboys in 1969. When I arrived, Bob had been the team's star defensive tackle for eight years, and he had single-handedly revolutionized the position.

It's been said that Bob Lilly was the greatest defensive tackle to ever play the game.

We were in awe of his superior athletic ability and skill—especially when watching him on game films. He was basically unstoppable. No one could block him. Guards would try to control him, but Bob would literally pick them up and throw them aside. The caliber of strength and quickness that he possessed was phenomenal.

In one game I remember seeing the guard pull in and the center trying to cut Lilly off. Bob, who stood 6′5″ tall and weighed about 260 pounds, literally jumped over the center!

His greatness on the field was challenged by many an opponent. Regardless of whether Bob was double-teamed or even triple-teamed, he'd still beat you. There were times when he didn't even confront the opposition at all. He would either jump over

*Bob Lilly (left) with Roger Staubach at the 2000 Pro Football Hall of Fame
ceremonies in Canton, Ohio.* PHOTO COURTESY OF THE DALLAS COWBOYS

them, go around them, or strategically outsmart them by making the play.

Even though Bob is physically a big man, he is a quiet and gentle person. I don't think he has a mean bone in his body. When he tackled an opponent, he did it in a clean manner. Bob always believed that it wasn't how hard you tackled but how well you tackled. From a quarterback's perspective, let's just say that I'm thankful we were both on the same team so I never had to experience the wrath of Bob Lilly.

In 1974 Bob retired from professional football. He had stood at the forefront of the Cowboys' Doomsday Defense for 14 years and helped the team to become world champions in Super Bowl VI.

In 1980 Bob was inducted into the Pro Football Hall of Fame. His presenter was his former coach and dear friend Tom Landry. During Tom's presentation, he told the Canton audience that Bob had been the greatest player he had ever coached.

Known affectionately as "Mr. Cowboy," Bob Lilly will forever be remembered as one of the elite who donned the Dallas Cowboys uniform.

—Roger Staubach

Acknowledgments

I would like to express my appreciation to Bob and Ann Lilly, whose countless hours of hard work made this book a reality; to Steve Sabol and Kathy Davis of NFL Films for their continued support of all my literary projects; to Mary Ann Wenger, NFL Films' Player and Talent Manager, for her knowledge and help with resources; to Roger Staubach for his contributions; and to Marc Cohen, Texas Christian University's Public Relations Director, for his help with supplying TCU archival resources.

.

Introduction

LIKE MANY OF THE NFL'S GREAT PLAYERS, Bob Lilly seemed larger than life. His style as a player and his character as a man converged into one heroic image.

It's easy to imagine Bob in another place in time—strolling ominously down the center of town with his gun sitting snugly in his holster, his badge glistening in the afternoon sun, and the bad guys waiting at the other end of town. At 6′5″ and 260 pounds, and with a hard frontier look about him, he could have easily played the part of marshal Matt Dillon in *Gunsmoke*. Instead Bob Lilly turned out to be a different kind of cowboy—a Dallas Cowboy.

This country boy from Throckmorton, Texas, also revolutionized the position of defensive tackle with a stunning combination of speed and strength.

It's been said that he was the greatest defensive tackle ever to put on a uniform. Known as "Mr. Cowboy," Lilly was the first draft pick in Dallas franchise history, the team's first All-Pro, the first Pro Bowl selection, the first Ring of Honor member, and the first Cowboy to be inducted into that elite franchise known as the Pro Football Hall of Fame. He was the first cornerstone of the Cowboys dynasty and the centerpiece of the feared Doomsday Defense of the 1960s that helped this expansion team reach championship heights. This country boy from Throckmorton, Texas, also revolutionized the position of defensive tackle with a stunning combination of speed and strength.

Lilly stood at the forefront as the Cowboys gained power and prestige. He was the unstoppable, immovable force of the Cowboys' defense. Opponents could neither contain him with a single player nor run away from him. Hall of Fame member Deacon Jones said, "[Bob] never gave up on a play, and that's what separates the guys that live in Canton from the guys that played this game. The ability to chase everything—every down—every 30 seconds."

Lilly left foes bent but not bloody—a trait not everyone appreciated. Bob's playing style was clean and pure without a trace of nastiness, but when this Cowboy was bushwhacked he sought frontier justice.

After Super Bowl V, Lilly and the Cowboys were sucker punched with the nickname "Next Year's Champions." Despite playing brilliantly in consecutive title game losses to the Packers and in a bitter defeat to the Colts in Super Bowl V, Lilly was lumped in with a team that was called heartless and gutless.

But in Super Bowl VI, next year had finally arrived. The Dolphins sank under Lilly's weight—as did the myth that the Cowboys were chokers. It seemed to take Lilly years to catch Bob Griese, and when he finally did, it was clear that the Cowboys' championship chase was about to end.

In a 24–3 win over Miami, the part-time photographer was responsible for the game's enduring image. Lilly was the team's oldest player, and he understood—perhaps more than anyone else—the significance of this victory.

When Bob completed his football career in 1974, the Dallas Cowboys were world champions and national heroes—they were "America's Team." But when he arrived in 1961, the Dallas Cowboys were nobody's team.

—Steve Sabol
President of NFL Films

A Cowboy's Life

First Quarter

The Early Years

1

My Dad, My Hero

I WAS BORN IN THE TOWN OF OLNEY, TEXAS, on July 26, 1939, but grew up in the small community of Throckmorton, Texas. Throckmorton is located about 120 miles west-northwest of the Dallas–Fort Worth area.

My dad, John Ernest "Buster" Lilly, has always been my most loyal and avid fan. My close relationship with him began at a very young age. He is the person responsible for introducing me to the game of football. But before I begin talking about the humble beginnings of my gridiron career, I would like to tell you a little more about my dad—his character, his values, and the kind of man that he was—for it was he who helped build the foundation for the man I would become.

My dad had a difficult upbringing. He was one of five children when his parents decided to divorce. His mom and siblings were so destitute that when he completed the seventh grade he was forced to drop out of school in order to contribute to the family's financial needs.

Dad had a motorcycle that he rode to and from work every day. One day while riding to work, a truck struck him down. The driver was intoxicated.

The blow was so violent that it completely crushed my dad's femur. The doctor had no alternative but to insert a steel plate into the leg where the femur had once been situated. Traction was not an option; after the surgery, Dad's leg shrank about an inch and a half. He was forced to wear an elevated shoe for the rest of his life.

His mom and siblings were so destitute that when he completed the seventh grade he was forced to drop out of school in order to contribute to the family's financial needs.

Shortly after the plate had been inserted into his thigh, the leg became badly infected at the insertion site. The doctor performed a surgical procedure on the leg, allowing it to drain. My dad continued to walk with a severe limp for many years.

It wasn't until I began playing for the Cowboys that my dad got a new lease on life. Dr. Marvin Knight was the team's doctor, and I told him about the ongoing problem with my dad's leg. Dr. Knight scheduled an appointment to evaluate the extremity of my dad's injury, and the findings indicated that immediate surgery was necessary.

The steel plate that had been inserted into my dad's thigh had become infected, and the infection had penetrated into the bone marrow. Dr. Knight removed the plate, but in order to totally clear the leg of infection, he had to literally chisel out part of my dad's femur. With the infection gone, his leg no longer required draining, and the healing process finally took over.

Throughout this entire ordeal my dad continued to be strong, both physically and spiritually. To this day, I believe those qualities contributed to his survival.

As a child I never realized how strong my dad really was until I visited him at his shop one day. He removed a Ford V-8 engine from a car with his bare hands because his winch had broken. From that point on I had a great deal of respect for my dad. I

made sure never to cross him and always behaved obediently…
well, except for one time.

We were eating at the dinner table. As the conversation of the
day commenced, my mother said something to me that I didn't
agree with. I responded by talking back to her. All
of a sudden I felt this pain in my head. My dad
had thumped me with his big finger and nearly
knocked me out! From that moment on, I knew
exactly who the boss was and that I had to play by
his rules. Needless to say, I never talked back to
my mom again.

He removed a Ford V-8 engine from a car with his bare hands because his winch had broken.

In 1947, when I was eight years old, my dad
took me to my first Throckmorton High School
football game. We attended every game that season, and I fell
in love with the sport. That same year he gave me my very first
football.

Dad did a lot of scouting for the Throckmorton football
coaches. One day Coach Mercer, the head football coach, gave
my dad an old, worn-out varsity football, and Dad brought the
ball home to me. I was so excited to receive that ball. The fact that
it was old and worn out didn't mean a thing. What was important
was that it was *my* football. From that day on, my dad would play
catch with me every chance he could. In sixth grade I finally got
the opportunity to go out for football. Back then I was tall and
very lanky. Our junior high football coach was Coach Morton.
He stood about 6´5″ and weighed about 250 pounds. A man that
size was considered quite big in those days.

One day, as he was demonstrating how to perform a forearm
block, he accidentally hit me in the nose. He hit me so hard that
I nearly executed a full backflip. You have to remember that
back then our helmets were made of leather, and the face mask

had not yet been invented. There was nothing blocking my face except my nose.

I ended up falling flat on my back. I hit my head on the ground so hard that my eyes literally crossed. The first thing that came to mind was, "I really don't think I want to play this game. It hurts too much!" But as I slowly pulled myself up off the ground and regained my bearings, I decided to give it one more try.

Because I was so tall and thin, I sometimes appeared awkward. Many times I can recall my dad telling my mom, "If that boy is planning to play football, he is going to have to grow some and fill out a little more."

It took me three years, but I finally did it. By ninth grade I was 6′4″ and weighed 180 pounds. I was still somewhat spindly, but I was very strong. I could run forever and never get tired. Football was still my first love, but my preference at that time was basketball. I was fortunate enough to play both.

> *By ninth grade I was 6′4″ and weighed 180 pounds.*

After each game I rode home with my parents. My dad was my biggest fan. His words were always encouraging. Whether I had played well or not, he always knew the right thing to say. He never spoke down to me or spoke in a negative manner.

One afternoon my parents came to see me play in an eighth-grade basketball game. As the clock was ticking down and after repeatedly yelling to my teammates, "Gimme the ball, gimme the ball!" the ball was finally in my hands. I guess I became a little anxious and somehow began dribbling toward our opponent's basket. It was similar to what happened to Vikings defensive end Jim Marshall during the Minnesota Vikings–San Francisco 49ers game years back.

Jim had recovered a fumble made by the 49ers' Billy Kilmer and ran 66 yards to the 49ers end zone, thinking he was scoring six points for the Vikings. Instead he ran in the opposite direction and into his *own* end zone. Jim ran into the end zone untouched and threw the ball away in jubilation. The ball landed out of bounds, which resulted in a safety for the 49ers. Fortunately for Marshall, his Vikings still won the game.

In my case, it was the second half of the game, and time was running out. I sprinted down the court, executed a great layup, and scored two points. But like Jim Marshall, it was two points for the *other team*. Unfortunately for us, and unlike the Vikings, we ended up losing our game.

At the end of the game, Coach Morton turned to me and said, "That was the dumbest thing I have ever seen!" He really didn't have to tell me that; I already knew it. I felt like I had let the team down.

Needless to say, I was pretty quiet on the drive home. I was not particularly proud of what I had done. That night my dad came into my room to say goodnight. He sat down on my bed and began to talk with me. He always found a way to bring up the game—whether we won or lost—without having to say a negative word.

In a soft-spoken voice he leaned over and said, "Son, did you get a little mixed up out there today?"

Not wanting to discuss it, but knowing that he meant well, I replied, "Yes, sir, I did."

He smiled, patted me on the shoulder, and said, "Well, don't worry about it. You're only in junior high school, and it's not going to have any effect on your career."

He always knew what to say and how to say it. I loved that quality in him.

My freshman year finally came, and I began playing football for the Throckmorton High School Greyhounds. It seemed as though I had waited a lifetime to be old enough to play for their team. I had a great freshman season, and by the time I became a sophomore, I weighed in at 210 pounds. I hadn't finished growing yet, though, and as a junior my weight increased to 220 pounds.

At that point my high school football and basketball careers began to take off. By the end of my junior year I was voted All-District and All-Bi-District in football, and I was All-District, All-Bi-District, and had an All-State honorable mention in basketball.

It is important to mention the loyalty, confidence, and dedication that my dad gave to me throughout my entire high school football career. He never missed any of my games—not one. Like the U.S. Postal Service, neither rain, nor sleet, nor snow kept him from attending. He wasn't only my dad; he was also my hero.

Toward the end of high school, some of the senior athletes began receiving letters regarding athletic scholarships. These letters of intent were sent by college coaches from around the country who had been scouting these boys with the hope of luring them to their own athletics programs.

My plan was to graduate from high school and join one of the branches of the armed forces. I was hoping to make a 25-year career out of the military and then retire. Upon retirement, I could do whatever I wanted with the remainder of my life.

But in December 1955 something happened that changed my plans drastically...and my life forever.

2

The Letter

IN DECEMBER 1955 I RECEIVED an unexpected letter from future Hall of Fame charter member Sammy Baugh, who was my dad's all-time football hero. Sammy played quarterback for Texas Christian University, where he was an All-American. While there, he picked up the nickname "Slingin' Sammy" from a Texas sportswriter.

During the Depression era of the mid-1930s, he placed TCU (which at that time was a very small college) on the national gridiron map. He led them to a muddy 1936 Sugar Bowl victory over Louisiana State by a score of 3–2 and a 16–6 win over Marquette in the 1937 Cotton Bowl, the first Cotton Bowl game ever played. He was also one of three MVPs of the game.

In 1937 he signed with the Washington Redskins for the unheard-of amount of $8,000, making him the highest-paid player on the team. He helped revolutionize the game of pro football by making the forward pass a routine play from scrimmage. His incredible accuracy led Washington to two NFL championships, and he is the only NFL player ever to lead the league in passing, punting, and interceptions in the same season.

At one point Sammy wasn't convinced that football was his best sport. He figured he could extend his professional sports career if he switched to baseball. Future Major League Baseball

Hall of Fame member Rogers Hornsby, then a scout for the St. Louis Cardinals, signed Sammy, who had also been an outstanding third baseman at TCU.

After being converted to shortstop, Sammy was farmed out to the minor league teams of Columbus and, later, Rochester. He also had trouble hitting a curveball. Realizing that he would never be the player that he hoped to be, Sammy returned to professional football.

After retiring from the NFL, Baugh accepted the head-coaching position at Hardin-Simmons University in 1955, which is where his unexpected letter comes in.

Upon reviewing my high school game films, Sammy wrote me a letter expressing interest in recruiting me for Hardin-Simmons, with the understanding that I had to have the grades to get in. Here's what the letter said:

> *Robert:*
>
> *Just wanted to let you know that as we were scouting your team, and while we were reviewing Throckmorton's game films, we were very impressed with your performance on the field.*
>
> *If you continue to improve and have a great senior year, we would like to offer you a football scholarship after graduation.*
>
> *P.S. In order to get into Hardin-Simmons, you will need to keep your grades up.*

Up to that point I had attended class (but without any enthusiasm), studied a little, and played sports. I was probably a C student, but after reading that letter it occurred to me that maybe the armed forces weren't my only choice after all. It wouldn't have been all that bad, but now I had the opportunity to attend college. If I could get my grades up, I would be the first one in my family to go.

I began to take studying seriously. It amazed me what I could accomplish by studying just one hour a day. I went from being an average student to an above-average student, and it really wasn't that difficult to achieve.

In 1956 I completed my junior year at Throckmorton High. That same year, the state of Texas suffered a severe drought—one that would continue for the next six years. My dad had always made his living in the farming business. Because he was nearing bankruptcy, our family was forced to make a life-changing decision.

Dad contacted his family in the Hermiston and Portland areas of Oregon and told them of his predicament. His family was more than happy to help him out and found work for him in a place called Pendleton, Oregon.

My dad sold everything we owned, including our home of seven years. He built a homemade trailer, and we took off for Oregon. I guess we resembled the *Beverly Hillbillies,* but with one big exception: the Lillys were moving to Pendleton, not Beverly Hills.

My dad sold everything we owned, including our home of seven years.

We finally settled into our new home—a home with neither a television nor a telephone. But still, it was home.

I completed my senior year at Pendleton High School. The transition from Throckmorton High to my new school was a little slow in the beginning, but I eventually made a whole new group of friends. But even more important, I became a starter on the Pendleton High Buckaroos football team.

I was now 17 years old, stood 6′5″, and weighed somewhere around 225–230 pounds. I ran a 10.6 in football cleats, which was considered to be a pretty good time for a guy of my size and weight.

I went out for football, basketball, and track and did well on every team. I was All-State in football, Second-Team All-State in basketball, and I made it to the state finals in track. I didn't win anything in track, but I sure enjoyed participating in the sport.

After graduating from Pendleton I received many college-scholarship offers, actually more for basketball than football. But in the end I chose football. And even though I chose not to attend Hardin-Simmons, I will always attribute my successes to Sammy Baugh, for it was his letter that gave me the incentive and the initiative to improve my grades and to attain a college scholarship.

Little did I realize that my connection to Sammy Baugh would continue for four more years and extend beyond his letter of 1955. I was offered a football scholarship to his alma mater, Texas Christian University.

3

Texas Christian University

MY GOD-GIVEN SKILL, ATHLETIC ABILITY, and good grades allowed me the privilege of picking the college of my choice. After reviewing various offers from numerous institutions, I decided to visit the University of Washington, Oregon State University, the University of Oregon, and Idaho. None of them seemed to gain my attention. Even Texas A&M coach Bear Bryant offered me a football scholarship, but I wasn't interested, nor did I take the time to visit the campus.

But in the summer of 1957 I received a penny postcard from Allie White, assistant coach to TCU head coach Abe Martin. White and Martin were prepared to offer me a four-year scholarship to play football at Texas Christian University. I decided to take them up on their offer and visit the Texas Christian University campus, and I eventually signed on as a TCU Frog, realizing my dream of playing football for TCU.

When I was a child my dad had taken me to TCU football games to watch his hero, Sammy Baugh, throw those long passes downfield.

When I was a child my dad had taken me to TCU football games to watch his hero, Sammy Baugh, throw those long passes downfield. Even after all those years, that purple blood was still flowing through my veins. But college life was quite different from what I had expected.

When I arrived at the TCU campus for the fall semester I didn't carry much with me—just one suitcase. My wardrobe consisted of a couple pairs of blue jeans, a few T-shirts, and one suit that I had worn to my high school graduation. Bringing a car to school wasn't even a consideration, as we didn't have the money for that type of luxury item.

> *The building I was supposed to live in had been condemned.*

Dorm living left a lot to be desired. The building I was supposed to live in had been condemned. Most of the screens and some of the windows had been knocked out by previous tenants. Even though this was a horrific excuse for suitable housing, it continued to accommodate the 34 members of TCU's freshman football team for the remainder of the season.

The building was finally torn down after my first year, but for the time that I was there, I felt pretty much at home—that is, until the rest of the student body showed up.

I had always assumed that the campus parking lots were for faculty and sports fans. Little did I know that the parking was reserved for college students! And to add insult to injury, the remaining student body arrived in fancy sports coats, penny loafers, and slacks. They sure made the rest of us feel poor. And we were.

Upon completion of my inaugural year, I finally began to enjoy college. Not only did I play football, but I got a summer job in the oil fields, made some good money, and bought some new clothes. My life was changing at a rapid pace, and I liked it.

TCU football had become my top priority. We had some pretty good teams while I was there. In my freshman year, my best afternoon came in the second-to-last game, which was with Southern Methodist University. Against SMU I blocked a punt, recovered two fumbles, and made 10 tackles as we held the Ponys rushers to minus-one yard.

Even though I didn't play varsity at that time, TCU won the 1957 Cotton Bowl against a Jim Brown–led Syracuse team in front of 68,000 spectators. A blocked extra-point attempt made the difference in the game and allowed TCU to win 28–27.

My varsity career began in 1958 when I was a sophomore. This is what the 1958 TCU *Football Media Guide* said about me:

> *Defensive Lineman No. 72*
> *Robert Lilly—6′4″, 235 pounds—Sophomore*
> *It would take a book to discuss the possibilities and assets this big guy has...a real top prospect, the best looking young tackle in years...potentially the finest soph tackle Abe has had...big, tough, and mobile, only lack of experience keeps him from being a polished performer...terrific as a freshman and in spring work... came to TCU from Pendleton, Oregon, where he was All-everything...hometown is Throckmorton...also was considered a top college prospect in basketball...keep your eye on this lad.*

That year TCU won the Southwest Conference championship with a 5–1 league mark and 8–2–1 overall record. Our only losses that year were to Iowa by a score of 17–0 and 20–13 to No. 18–ranked SMU. TCU would not win another conference title until 2005, when it captured the Mountain West Conference championship. The Horned Frogs climbed as high as No. 6 in the national rankings in 1958 after opening the season with a 42–0 win at Kansas. TCU closed the year ranked ninth after tying undefeated No. 6 Air Force 0–0 in the Cotton Bowl.

The Cotton Bowl was played on January 1, 1959. Just prior to the game 20 inches of snow had fallen on the field. The problem wasn't the snow; it was that the groundskeepers at the Cotton Bowl never removed it. It just sat there until it finally melted. This left the field extremely muddy and put both Air Force and TCU at a great disadvantage.

During the game Air Force attempted three field goals, and TCU attempted two. Neither team was successful. The game ended in a 0–0 tie, which didn't leave a very good taste in anybody's mouth.

The 1959 season posted an 8–3 overall record while the team's 5–1 league mark tied Arkansas and Texas for the Southwestern Conference title. The following is an excerpt from the 1959 *Football Media Guide*:

> *Defensive Lineman No. 72*
> *Robert Lilly—6´4˝, 240 pounds—Junior*
> *One of the top all-around performers on the 1959 team and could have another great season...along with All-American Don Floyd on the other side, these two could give TCU the best pair of starting tackles in the nation...he doesn't have to take his hat off to anyone, and if desire holds up will make a top bid for all honors...had great year for first season on varsity...started but one game, but Abe liked him on second unit, to help give needed punch there (this is one reason the second team will be weaker in 1959)...but when seeded with first-team defense he was rushed into contest...size and strength gives him advantage over the smaller opponents in the line...as Allie says, "This guy came equipped like a new automobile—with overdrive, air conditioning, power*

*pack, and everything one would want."... [He] was top
star at Pendleton, Oregon, winning All-America honors
in football and All-State in basketball...decided on TCU,
as folks moved back to Texas...players call him "Tiger"
and it seems appropriate...[he] never makes a mistake.*

The campaign was highlighted by a 14–9 victory over second-ranked Texas in Austin. TCU also posted shutouts of Baylor and SMU.

At the end of the season TCU earned a trip to Houston to play against Clemson in the first-ever Bluebonnet Bowl. Although we lost 23–7, I was still awarded Lineman of the Game. TCU closed out the season ranked seventh nationally.

After the season the following article appeared in the 1960 TCU *Football Media Guide*:

Unanimous Preseason All-America Choice

Robert Lilly is the best TCU tackle ever! Strength, agility, ability, the great Purple cloud, the best tackle in the USA.

The adjectives ring long and loud, and each seems to appropriately describe Robert Lilly, who, at 6´5″ and 250 pounds, is the biggest Frog of them all. Appropriately called "Tiger" by the players, this Purple giant, who has been known to lift sports cars, is expected to be the best among the nation's collegiate linemen this fall.

He is that good. His coaches, teammates, opponents, and even the top professional scouts adhere to that.

Selected on the numerous preseason All-America teams, the former Texas and Oregon schoolboy great seems headed for a great campaign in 1960. From his first freshman test in 1957 until the Bluebonnet Bowl game last December, where he was chosen by the writers as the outstanding lineman of the contest, his play has been more than superb.

"He is simply the best lineman I have ever coached," says his head coach, Abe Martin. "What tremendous physical and football ability in one neat package! He has made some outstanding plays while at TCU, and he'll make more, and I am convinced that he will be ahead of the class when the nation's greats are picked at the end of the season. If he has a flaw, we don't know it."

Martin's line coach, Allie White, who was a great tackle on the Purples' only national championship team in 1938, goes even further.

"He is the best tackle or lineman we have ever had at TCU. And I don't think anyone in America has one like him. In the last half of the 1959 season, he was great. His possibilities are unlimited."

And then there was one of Lilly's teammates who came up with the quip, "If I was as big and strong as Lilly, I would charge folks just to live."

Lilly did have a splendid year in 1959. With All-America tackle Don Floyd as a teammate, it was hard for the big youngster to grab any of the limelight. Though it was apparent at the end of the campaign that Lilly belonged in the same class with Floyd, who was a consensus selection. Both TCU tackles were unanimous All-Conference choices, a rare feat in the Southwest Conference.

Robert's play against LSU, Pittsburgh, Baylor, Texas, Rice, SMU, and Clemson in the Bluebonnet Bowl impressed all, drawing raves from both the opposing players and coaches. He recovered seven fumbles and averaged at least eight tackles a game.

But his best afternoons seemed to come in the two final games with SMU and Clemson. Against SMU he blocked a punt, recovered two fumbles, and made ten tackles as the Frogs held the Ponys rushers to minus-one yard. Then in the loss to Clemson, Lilly was everywhere on the field, in a greater display than either TCU's Floyd or Clemson's Lou Cordileone, both of whom were chosen on 1959 All-America teams.

"I love the game," said Big Robert. "It gives me a chance to excel against others. I think we'll have a good season this fall, but it looks like a tough schedule. But I think we will do okay."

Lilly played ball at Throckmorton, Texas, before his family moved to Pendleton, Oregon, where he was a standout for two years. He was an All-American and was the state javelin champion in track.

A three-cent stamp and a hometown buddy—Max Hibbits, who was a center on the Frogs' varsity—are credited with luring the big fellow back to the Lone Star State.

Lilly should become TCU's seventh All-American tackle at the close of the 1960 season. His coaches and teammates plan for him to be there.

Robert also plans to accept the challenge in grand style.

Throughout my gridiron career at TCU, I was voted All–Southwest Conference twice and Consensus All-American in my senior year, but I truly believe that the Lineman of the Game

I truly believe that the Lineman of the Game award gave me that extra boost of notoriety that I needed to attract the pro scouts.

award gave me that extra boost of notoriety that I needed to attract the pro scouts. Whatever it was, it worked.

That same year the Dallas Texans and the Dallas Cowboys franchises came into existence. I was drafted number one by the Cowboys and number two by the Texans.

With my collegiate career behind me, I was now ready to enter what was known as "the lucrative world of pro football."

Little did I know that the journey I was about to embark upon would be one that would forever impact my life.

Second Quarter

From
Nobody's Team
to America's Team

4

A Cowboy First

IN 1961 I BECAME THE FIRST-EVER DRAFT pick of the Dallas Cowboys. Among my God-given gifts were pass-rushing skills and the ability to shatter plays using agility and instinct. It was a dream come true for this farm boy from Throckmorton, Texas.

That same year Major League Baseball witnessed one of the most amazing performances ever as Yankees teammates Mickey Mantle and Roger Maris battled it out to surpass the all-time, single-season home-run record, which was set in 1927 by another Yankees slugger named Babe Ruth. The Babe hit 60, and Mantle and Maris were competing for number 61. Maris finally passed the Bambino on the last day of the season against the Red Sox's Tracy Stallard.

The Yankees also won the World Series that year by beating their rivals, the Cincinnati Reds. I happened to catch one of the TV interviews with Mickey Mantle and was extremely impressed by the glitz and glamour provided by the media and the Yankees organization.

Mantle was posing for the cameras in front of his huge, fully carpeted, oversized locker. Inscribed above were the initials *MM*. His pinstriped uniforms were neatly hung up inside.

With his Yankees cap tilted back on his head and a big cigar in his mouth, Mantle relaxed in a large chair in front of his locker while the media asked questions, flashed a multitude of lights from their cameras, and enveloped him with microphones.

That single event paralleled my perception of myself as an NFL player and as the number one draft choice of the new franchise. But I would soon realize that, unlike the New York Yankees, the Dallas Cowboys would have to wait many years before they would achieve that kind of glamour and glory.

In my rookie season I signed with the Cowboys for $11,500 with a $2,500 bonus. Of course, in those days we didn't have agents to help us with contracts.

I immediately used the bonus money to buy my first car. It was a Chevy Corvair. It was all I could afford at the time with the bonus money I had received. It was a nice little car with good gas mileage, and that's basically all I was looking for.

I got into my car, reviewed my directions, and was on my way to Dallas's Burnett Field for my first meeting with Coach Tom Landry and the Dallas Cowboys.

Within a block of the dealership, the car broke down. Apparently a couple of bolts had fallen out of the engine because of improper installation. The owner of the dealership upgraded me to a new car—one that was five hundred dollars more than the Corvair.

I was thankful for the upgrade, but I had lost quite a bit of road time by having to exchange cars. I knew I was running late and was afraid of creating a bad first impression with Coach Landry.

I expected Burnett Field to be something like the Yankees facility that I saw during the interview with Mickey Mantle. I figured the Cowboys facility would be as impressive, if not more so, but when I arrived at the stadium it wasn't quite what I had expected.

There before me stood an old, abandoned, minor league park. The deserted parking lot had seen better days and was now cracked and broken. I decided to drive to the back of the stadium to look for signs of life. There I saw a few cars parked on an old gravel road.

I searched for a way to enter the building, but all I could find was a cavernous opening, which I assumed represented a poor pretext for a doorway. I went in and checked it out.

The facility was extremely dark and hollow inside, like some medieval castle. Old and rusted World War II lightbulbs covered by army-green plates provided the lighting.

I knew I was running late and was afraid of creating a bad first impression with Coach Landry.

As I continued making my way through this archaic structure, I suddenly heard voices coming from one of the rooms. I soon realized that this was where the meeting was being held. Considerably late, I was a little intimidated about walking in.

As I entered the room, Coach Landry was writing on the board. He stopped writing, turned around and faced the class, and with that blank, stone-cold face said, "I want to introduce you to Bob Lilly, one of your new teammates. Now, Bob, once we start our regular season and begin training camp, there will be a $50 fine if you are late. And every time you're late thereafter, the fine will double."

Thoroughly embarrassed and with nowhere to hide, I focused my eyes to the ground and found my way to an empty seat.

Coach Landry valued consistency in demeanor, preparation, and execution more than anything else in life. He truly believed that to do something, and to do it right, you had to be consistent. Everyone had to know his place and then execute correctly. This obsession with consistency was simply known as the "Landry Credo": Faith. Training. A Goal. The Will.

Coach Landry turned back around, faced the blackboard, and began writing a list of his priorities in life. He wrote them in this order: *God, family, and football.*

Every guy—and I mean *every guy*—in that room turned around and looked at each other in amazement. We all thought the same thing: *Coach has his priorities backward.* In the minds of the players, the order should have been football, family, and God. It took a while for us to get it, but in the long run we found that Coach knew what he was talking about and, as usual, he was right.

After the meeting, we headed off to the locker room to get our equipment. I was handed an old, dilapidated game jersey to wear in practice. It had holes all over it from offensive linemen's fingers grabbing and pulling at it. The jerseys were so bad that I thought the club might be in a bind for money.

Jack Eskridge, our equipment manager, told us on the first day of practice to be sure to hang up our clothing and cleats on the pipes above the lockers or on the nails inside of the lockers. He firmly stipulated that nothing was to be left on the floor. If we chose to do otherwise, then we would find ourselves sharing our lockers with the local rats who would infest the facility after we had gone. If you left your shoes, shoulder pads, or anything else that was made of leather on the floor, the rats would eat it.

Jack would leave rat poison out in the locker room before he left at night. The next morning we would find dead rats all over the place. Over time, their systems acclimated to the toxin, and it no longer had an effect on them.

Other negatives about Burnett Field were that the showers never got hot, the building was always cold—due to the lack of central heating—and it didn't have a meeting room large enough to accommodate the entire team. We were forced to drive to the

AAA building in Dallas for all of our meetings. At the conclusion of our daily chalk talk, we would have to drive 20–30 minutes back to Burnett Field for practice.

Coach Landry first played me at the defensive end position on the left side. I never felt completely comfortable playing on that side. I caught myself always watching for reverses, bootlegs, and traps instead of using my natural instincts and going for the ball.

> *The next morning we would find dead rats all over the place.*

Halfway through my third year, Coach moved me to the right tackle position. He felt I was better suited to play there because I had good movement and agility. I no longer had to wait for the play to develop as I did when I was playing end. I believe he made the right decision for me. Besides, my football hero was Baltimore great Gino Marchetti, who was a future Hall of Fame defensive tackle. I emulated his style and hoped to someday be as great a player as he was.

Tackle was a natural position for me. I was right in the middle of the action—having to think quickly and move quickly. I loved it from the very first day.

In 1963 the Dallas Texans moved to Kansas City and the Cowboys moved into the Texans' former facility. The new location was close to Clint Murchison's office building, and Mr. Murchison was the owner of the Cowboys. The team was immediately convinced that this new facility, unlike Burnett Field, had little chance of being infested with rats.

We had this great locker room complete with doors! Imagine that! We even had bright lights, big shower areas, and a nice training room. We were beginning to look like a real professional football team. Things were starting to look up. Maybe my dream of having a locker like Mickey Mantle's wasn't as far fetched as I thought.

About this same time our defense started to improve and develop. We had become one of the better defenses in the league and continued that streak throughout the majority of my career. The man responsible for developing that Cowboys legacy is none other than Coach Tom Landry, whom I consider to be a man for all seasons.

5

Coach Tom Landry:
A Man for All Seasons

BORN THOMAS WADE LANDRY in Mission, Texas, on September 11, 1924, Tom Landry was the middle child of Ruth and Ray Landry. Ray was an auto mechanic and volunteer fireman. Tom's two older siblings were brother Robert and sister Ruthie.

When Tom was just a small child, he developed a speech impediment that caused him to become self-conscious and somewhat shy—a characteristic he never seemed to overcome. As he grew older he earned money by selling newspapers and working as a caddie. His dream was to become a cowboy, and he loved to go to the movies with his friends and watch the old Westerns. Little did he know that his dream of becoming a cowboy would someday become a reality—although this cowboy would lead a football team, not a horse.

Tom's football career began in the sandlots of Mission. He went on to play the quarterback position at Mission High School, where he was awarded two All–South Texas designations. His skill, intelligence, and diversity in the game earned him a place in the Texas High School All-Star Game and a football scholarship to play for the Longhorns at the University of Texas in Austin. At the university, Tom majored in industrial engineering.

While Tom was away at college, his brother Robert enlisted in the U.S. Army Air Corps soon after the attack on Pearl Harbor and immediately went into its pilots' training program. While flying his B-17 to England, his plane disappeared over the North Atlantic near Iceland. A few weeks later the family received a fateful call—Robert was no longer missing in action; he had now been officially declared dead.

Robert's death had an incredible impact on Tom's life. That November, just a couple of months after his 18th birthday, Tom interrupted his education to enlist in the army reserves and applied for pilot training. He earned his wings and a commission as a second lieutenant and became the copilot of a B-17 Flying Fortress bomber in the 860th Bomb Squadron. While stationed in Debach, England, he was assigned to the 493rd Bomb Group. From November 1944 to April 1945 Tom flew 30 missions. He and his entire crew miraculously survived after crashing their plane in Belgium following a bombing run over Czechoslovakia. I believe that God was watching over Tom, because it was the Lord's plan that he would become one of the great innovators of the game of professional football.

Landry returned to UT in 1946 and continued his college and football careers. He played defensive back and fullback for the Longhorns and appeared in two victorious New Year's Day bowl games—the 1948 Sugar Bowl and the 1949 Orange Bowl. He became known as "Terrific Tommy Landry" to the local sportswriters.

At the time, the quarterback for the Longhorns was none other than future Hall of Fame member Bobby Layne. In those days the college teams and the pro teams were close—the coaches all knew each other. I had the opportunity to play against Bobby when he was with the Steelers in 1961, the year before he retired.

He was as good and tough as the image he portrayed. We ended up losing that game 37–7.

Former assistant coach Blair Cherry took over the head coaching position in 1947. He announced to the team that they were going to go with a pro-style offense. That meant switching their offense from a single wing to a T formation.

Coach Cherry took Bobby with him to the Chicago Bears' training camp to learn the new offense. There, coach George Halas and his first-string quarterback, Sid Luckman, taught Bobby everything he needed to know. Coach Landry's assignment that year was to learn the new offense because he would be the backup for Layne. Realizing that he wouldn't get much playing time with Bobby at the helm, Tom became a defensive back and backup running back. It was difficult for Tom to give up the quarterback position, but his competitive nature was a guarantee that he would be playing on that gridiron regardless of the position.

The year 1947 was also a turning point in Tom's life. His greatest highlight of that year didn't involve gridiron glory; it was meeting his future wife, Alicia, also a student at UT.

Tom's last season at UT was in 1948. Heading into the Orange Bowl, the team's record was 6–3–1. Texas was matched up against eighth-ranked Georgia with Georgia favored to win easily. But Landry and the Longhorns had a much different scenario in mind.

Due to player injuries, Tom played offense and defense and even punted. While filling in at fullback he carried the ball 17 times for 117 yards as the Longhorns trounced the Bulldogs 41–28.

Upon completing his final semester exam on the morning of January 28, 1949, Tom drove with Alicia to Houston, where they were married.

Tom graduated from the University of Texas in 1949, and later, in 1952, he earned a bachelor of science degree in industrial engineering from the University of Houston.

Pro Career

After graduating from the University of Texas in 1949, Tom became a defensive back and punter for the Yankees of the old All-America Conference. After his first year, the Yankees franchise dissolved due to financial difficulties, and Landry became the property of the Giants.

From 1950 to 1959, first as a player and later as a genius of defensive innovations, Tom Landry built the New York Giants into one of the NFL's most feared teams. At 6′1″ and 195 pounds, he emerged as a defensive back, kick returner, and punter—and even filled in at the quarterback position. Those days at the University of Texas as a backup quarterback to Bobby Layne had finally paid off.

Tom Landry built the New York Giants into one of the NFL's most feared teams.

He was also selected All-Pro in 1954. Tom wasn't really that fast or strong, but his ability to analyze and anticipate what the opposition would do next was second to none.

Tom's coach, Steve Owen, once told him, "The best offense can be built around ten basic plays, the best defense on two. All the rest is razzle-dazzle, egomania, and box office." Coach Landry never forgot that and passed that knowledge on to his coaches and players.

He played in the Pro Bowl after the 1954 season but always leaned toward coaching. In 1956, after two seasons as a player/coach, Tom became the Giants' full-time defensive coach. In his first season, he devised a new defensive alignment called the 4-3 defense. He took Sam Huff out of the standard five-man defensive front line and placed him behind the linemen. Landry originally developed this flex defense to stop Paul Brown's Cleveland Browns offense. Eventually the new defense became successful throughout the NFL, and each team developed its own variation of the flex.

Landry also coined the term *red dog*, which he used for blitzes, and he was the first coach to call defensive audibles by calling signals from the sideline. He was destined to take the game to a higher, more intellectual level. Giants head coach Jim Lee Howell called his assistant coach "the greatest defensive coordinator in the game today."

Tom Landry changed the nature of pass coverage forever, and as a result, the Giants' defensive unit was the first team in NFL history to be praised, respected, and honored by their fans. As former commissioner Bert Bell boasted, "The fans love the defense!"

Tom always felt that defense was the most challenging part of the game. He used to say, "The offensive has its plays diagrammed for them and knows ahead of time exactly what it has to do. On the other hand, the defense must constantly anticipate and react. On defense, you have to accept the fact that you're going to give the other guy the first shot, the initial advantage." Figuring out a way to take some of that advantage away was always the most intriguing part of the game for Landry.

> *Tom Landry changed the nature of pass coverage forever.*

While Landry was running the Giants' defense, future Packers coach and Hall of Fame member Vince Lombardi ran the offense. Their loyalty to their given units contributed to the appearance of the Giants in three NFL championship games in four years.

In 1956 the Giants beat the Bears 47–7 but were defeated by the Baltimore Colts in both 1958 and 1959.

Not only did Landry coach with Lombardi, one of the greatest minds in the National Football League, but he also had the benefit of playing with gridiron greats like Frank Gifford and Kyle Rote, and he coached players like All-Pro linebacker Sam Huff and All-Pro defensive tackle Rosey Grier. His commuter buddy from Connecticut was a man whose name would become synonymous with *Monday Night Football* and who was "the sports announcer that everyone loved to hate," Howard Cosell. These associations and friendships with some of the greatest players and coaches in football history, coupled with Landry's intelligence and drive, turned him into the most successful coach in the history of the game. But even he could not have predicted that he was going to be given the unique opportunity to create a brand-new NFL team and take them to the pinnacle of success.

6

The Birth of the Cowboys

IN THE LATE 1950S THE NFL BEGAN TO TALK of expanding to other cities. Chicago Bears owner George Halas was head of the league's expansion committee. The committee wanted to add two new franchises to the league and have them ready to play by the start of the 1961 season. One team would be in Dallas and the other would be in either Houston or Minneapolis.

When AFL founder Lamar Hunt got word of the NFL expansion, he immediately announced that play would begin for the 1960 season in eight cities, including Dallas and Houston. With that news, Halas drove the NFL's committee to begin expansion immediately. He didn't want the AFL to be the first to mark their territory in the Texas gridiron market.

Not all NFL owners were eager to expand. George Preston Marshall of the Washington Redskins felt that there was no need for expansion. Things were fine the way they were, and besides, expansion could only hurt the league—so he thought. But then Marshall also thought that African Americans had no place in the NFL, refusing to sign black players even after such stars as Ollie Matson, Jim Brown, and Lenny Moore had broken into the league in the 1950s.

Halas, on the other hand, didn't see it the same way. He went ahead and recruited for financial backing for a Dallas team—and got it.

A 36-year-old Texas oil millionaire by the name of Clint Murchison Jr. and his partners bought the new team for $600,000, subject to the league's approval at the meeting in January.

Due to the fact that the Murchison team lacked administrative football experience, Halas called in his friend Tex Schramm to sign on as general manager of the new franchise. Schramm had been the general manager of the Los Angeles Rams but retired in 1957 to work as a studio executive with CBS Sports. As a television executive in 1960, Tex was the man responsible for the first-ever telecast of the Winter Olympics in Squaw Valley, California. Schramm employed Walter Cronkite as one of his news anchors.

With his new job title, Schramm went head-hunting for a coach to head up his new franchise. At this same time, Landry returned to Texas to meet with another Texas oilman, a man by the name of Bud Adams. Adams had his eye on Landry to coach his new AFL franchise in Houston.

Coach Landry agreed to meet with him to discuss the ground-level plans for the team. Before leaving the meeting, Tom said he would think about the offer, but in reality, he and Alicia felt it was time for him to get out of football and into a job that would provide more security for his family.

But the offers didn't stop. Wellington Mara, co-owner of the New York Giants, called Landry to let him know that he had agreed to allow Murchison and company to approach him regarding the head-coaching position at Dallas, but first he had some other news that he wanted to run by him.

Coach Jim Lee Howell of the Giants was planning to retire soon. Wellington asked Landry if he would be interested in the head-coaching position with the Giants. Tom and Alicia had already decided that the '59 season would be Tom's last year in New York. They were ready to return home to Texas.

Although Landry had all but written off the idea of returning to football, he couldn't stop thinking about the Dallas position. After all, the team would be located in Dallas, so he and Alicia could live year-round in one home instead of commuting back and forth from New York, and at the same time Tom could begin building his business. But most important, his family would have stability for the first time ever—not to mention that Tom could stay in football a little while longer.

Although Landry had all but written off the idea of returning to football, he couldn't stop thinking about the Dallas position.

Tom liked the way Tex did business, the way he handled personnel, and his knowledge of scouting, which was something Tom knew little about.

Tex called up his old colleague from the Rams, Gil Brandt, and together they would build the Cowboys scouting system. Tex also promised Landry that he could hire his own coaching staff and would have the last word when it came to making decisions about all player personnel issues. Having the same goals and objectives, Tom took Tex up on his offer to coach the new franchise.

Tex was brilliant at marketing strategies. In order to get more fans into the stands, Schramm proposed that Dallas have tryouts and select a group of good-looking, sexy cheerleaders in skimpy outfits and incorporate them into the marketing scheme of the organization. Of course, his inspiration took off like wildfire at Dallas and with the other NFL teams. The rest is history.

Tex's background and experience in the world of football was definitely a plus, so on December 27, 1959, Landry accepted and signed the five-year personal-service contract that paid him $34,500 a season.

Coach Landry knew that this job wasn't going to be easy. Building a professional football team from scratch would take a great deal of patience, knowledge, and time. He said as much to the press. But Tom still had one more obstacle to overcome.

In January 1960 the NFL team owners met in Miami to vote on the new Dallas franchise. Clint Murchison and his team waited nervously outside the meeting-room doors. Little did they know that their stay in Miami would be far longer than had been expected. There were still a few owners—one in particular, the Redskins' George Preston Marshall—who were adamantly against expansion.

Building a professional football team from scratch would take a great deal of patience, knowledge, and time.

The official approval of the new team was only one of two issues that needed to be decided, as a successor to the commissioner had yet to be named and voted upon. Commissioner Bert Bell had died of a heart attack on October 11, 1959, while watching his two formerly owned teams, the Philadelphia Eagles and the Pittsburgh Steelers, battle it out at Philadelphia's Franklin Field. Pro football had been Mr. Bell's lifelong passion, so passing away at this particular NFL game seemed an appropriate end.

The voting wasn't easy. Seven days would pass before a decision was made. The commissioner voting remained deadlocked throughout 22 rounds of voting. In the meantime George Halas refused to commit for fear of losing support on either side for his proposal of franchise expansion.

With another deadlock imminent, Browns owner Paul Brown and Giants co-owner Wellington Mara together proposed a candidate. Their choice: Alvin "Pete" Rozelle—the Los Angeles Rams' young general manager and former colleague of Tex Schramm.

Rozelle was young and hadn't made any enemies within the league. On the 23rd and final ballot, Alvin Rozelle was voted in as the NFL's new commissioner; he would lead the league into the next generation of players and management.

But the league's next order of business, the expansion vote, would take another two days to decide. And it's hard to imagine that eventually it all came down to a song.

The whole thing started when George Preston Marshall fired his band director, who had composed the Redskins' official fight song, "Hail to the Redskins." Upset with Marshall's decision, the band director sold the copyright of the song to one of Marshall's rivals. That rival turned out to be an attorney for Clint Murchison, who had just purchased the Cowboys organization.

Finally, after two days of angry debates over whether or not to expand, George Marshall said he would agree to the Dallas expansion on one condition: Clint Murchison's lawyer had to agree to give him back the rights to "Hail to the Redskins."

Clint Murchison's $600,000 dream of owning a team in Dallas was finally a reality.

The condition was granted, and on January 28, 1960, Dallas was voted into the NFL. It was also Tom and Alicia's 11th wedding anniversary. They couldn't wish for a better omen than that.

Clint Murchison's $600,000 dream of owning a team in Dallas was finally a reality. Story has it that Murchison's attitude about Marshall resulted in the intense rivalry the Cowboys have had with the Redskins all these years. Of course, it was strictly personal on Murchison's part.

7

Putting the Team Together

CLINT AND HIS ASSOCIATES may have been granted their franchise, but acquiring good players to make up a team that could compete within the NFL was another story.

Lucky for the Cowboys, George Halas had foreseen the problem before it was too late. Due to the fact that his new team started after the college draft was over, Halas asked Tex Schramm to persuade owner Clint Murchison to sign two collegiate stars to personal-service contracts.

The first was a 6′3″, 210-pound two-time All-American quarterback out of SMU by the name of Joseph Don Meredith and the second, an overlooked 5′10″, 204-pound running back from the University of New Mexico named Don Perkins. Aware of Dallas's intentions, the other NFL owners were careful not to draft Meredith or Perkins. Just to be sure that there would be no future repercussions from the other owners, George Halas himself used his third-round pick in order to secure the rights to Meredith. He then traded those rights to Dallas for a Cowboys' third-round pick in the 1961 draft.

Still desperate to find an undrafted college player with potential, Tex began to look for players under unusual circumstances. He found one in a 6′3″, 243-pound tackle named Byron Bradfute.

Bradfute, a big lineman from Abilene Christian University, was thrown out of school for drinking beer. He ended up completing his senior year at Southern Mississippi. Tex didn't have any moral hang-ups and was concerned only with signing talent and building a winning team.

The AFL Chargers drafted Bradfute in the 17th round, but he decided to sign with Dallas because it would allow him to be closer to his family in Texas.

Next the Cowboys picked up Jake Crouthamel, a 6′0″, 195-pound running back out of Dartmouth; Jim Doran, a 6′2″, 201-pound end from the Lions; and Frank Clarke, a 6′1″, 215-pound end from the Browns.

With no time to spare, Schramm hired Gil Brandt and sent him all over the country to scout for talent.

Before the National Football League employed Brandt as the Cowboys' vice president of player personnel, he had worked as a baby photographer in Wisconsin.

Brandt first met Tex in the 1950s when he served as a part-time scout for the Los Angeles Rams. Back then, Tex was the general manager of the Southern California team. When Schramm took the position of general manager with the new Dallas franchise, he hired Gil to serve as the Cowboys' chief talent scout.

Over the years Brandt utilized his expertise to pioneer many of the scouting techniques that are still used in the NFL. Two of those techniques include computer analysis of prospects and converting basketball players and track stars into football players.

Following Schramm's instructions, Brandt grabbed a handful of NFL free-agent contracts and signed all the nondrafted hopefuls he could find in order to field Dallas's first team; but the problem was that the team desperately needed experienced players. Fielding a team of college rookies was definitely out of the question.

Again Halas stepped in, and again the owners were unhappy with what he proposed. He had requested that each NFL team give up a limited number of veteran players to Dallas. That wasn't going to happen, so Tex and Tom decided to personally take their case to the next owners' meeting in Los Angeles.

Tom was never comfortable with public speaking but was forced to plead his case in front of the owners, who were steadily losing their patience with the new team. The decision was not good.

According to the decision, each owner was allowed to protect 25 of his 34 players.

In those days there were 34 men on each team's roster. According to the decision, each owner was allowed to protect 25 of his 34 players, leaving only nine "unprotected" players on each team. Out of the nine, Dallas was allowed to pick only three from each team. And to make matters worse, Dallas had only 24 hours to make their selections. After that the deal was off.

Did I mention that out of the $600,000 that Clint Murchison paid for the club, $100,000 was for the franchise and half a million went to the other NFL owners for a roster of players who had definitely seen better days?

Coach did the best he could with the 36 players he had chosen. He had a receiver, Frank Clarke; a 6'0", 182-pound veteran backup quarterback, Don Heinrich, whom he had known from his days with the Giants; and a 6'2", 221-pound linebacker named Jerry Tubbs, who was gladly released by 49ers coach Red Hickey due to irreconcilable differences.

Coach Landry's ability to analyze and construct great strategies for both offense and defense was critical to developing the Dallas organization. His personal timeline projected that the Cowboys franchise would have a winning program within the next three years.

Coach Landry's ability to analyze and construct great strategies for both offense and defense was critical to developing the Dallas organization.

With running back Don Perkins and quarterback Don Meredith, Coach knew he had a good chance, but Meredith would need a little help in the beginning. Tom was able to talk former Redskins quarterback Eddie LeBaron out of retiring after the 1959 season. This in turn led to another unforeseen problem. Washington still owned the rights to LeBaron. If Dallas wanted him, it was going to cost the club dearly. And cost them it did. Washington was granted the Cowboys' 1961 first-round draft pick.

Tom was in a difficult situation, but Meredith needed to learn the tricks of the game, and the diminutive 5'7", 168-pound LeBaron was just the one to show him. It was a price Coach was willing to pay.

With the 1960 preseason about to begin, the Cowboys were still down on their luck. Don Perkins suffered an injury in the College All-Star Game, ending his season before it even started.

The veterans, who were searching for lost youth and one more autumn season of glory, resented having to learn complex offensive and defensive strategies; while the young, inexperienced rookies were thoroughly confused by the complexity of the system and were no match for future Hall of Fame running back greats like the Browns' Jim Brown and Green Bay's Paul Hornung and Jim Taylor.

Tom once told me a story about a 1960 preseason game against the Giants that involved rookie quarterback Don Meredith. Here's what he said:

Meredith brought the team to the line of scrimmage and noticed middle linebacker Sam Huff lined up in the exact spot where the play was supposed to go. When Don changed the play by calling an audible, both Huff and defensive lineman Rosey Grier immediately shifted to another gap. So Don audibled another play, and this time the two defensive ends, Robustelli and Jim Katcavage, moved. It was as if the veteran Giants could read Don's mind. He hurriedly tried to think of yet another play to call, stuttered, swore out loud, and disgustedly called, "Timeout!" The entire veteran Giants defense broke out laughing as Don shook his head in total frustration.

Speaking of frustration, there was nothing more frustrating than the practice facility at Burnett Field. One winter's day during that freezing 1960 season the facility had gotten so cold that someone in the training room lit the contents of a trash can on fire just to warm up the place.

Sometime during the middle of practice one of the players noticed smoke billowing out from underneath the stands. Tom and his assistant coaches dropped what they were doing and immediately rushed over to the area to put out the flames. Funny thing, though, the players didn't pitch in. They just stood there and watched, hoping that their luck would hold and the entire facility would burn down.

The 1960 inaugural season was about to begin, but on game day the fans didn't exactly come out to the ballpark en masse. The few that did show up were pretty much scattered throughout the stadium. When the rains came, they huddled underneath the stadium shelter, and it looked like the stands were completely deserted.

That first year was the worst year that Coach would ever experience. The Cowboys were 0–10 when they left for New York to play the Giants in the next-to-last game of the season. The game ended in a 31–31 tie.

When the team returned to Dallas's Love Field, they were welcomed home by two lonely fans and a sign that proclaimed, "Well done, Cowboys!"

Dallas brought the 1960 season to a close with a loss to Detroit, finishing the year with an 0–11–1 record, the worst the NFL had seen in 18 years.

8

Stepping It Up

THE 1961 SEASON SAW THE DALLAS COWBOYS change training camps as we arrived at St. Olaf College in Northfield, Minnesota.

Because of the draft deals that were made in the Cowboys' inaugural year, talented players were few and far between. Remember we had given up our first-round draft pick to the Redskins for quarterback Eddie LeBaron and our third-round pick to the Bears when Halas secured Don Meredith for the Cowboys so no other team could draft him. Also, a new expansion club had arrived on the scene.

They called themselves the Minnesota Vikings and, because they were the new kids on the block, they were awarded the first pick in every round of the draft—an advantage that was denied the Cowboys before the start of their first season in the NFL.

Of course, I was the first draft choice of the Cowboys that year—in reality, the Cowboys' first draft choice ever. We were fortunate enough to obtain the rights to former Chicago Bears linebacker Chuck Howley. The 6′3″, 228-pound Howley had been sidelined with an injury since the '59 season but was now healed up and ready to play for us.

Howley, Jerry Tubbs, and I had become the foundation of a respectable defense for our team, but Coach knew that he really had to concentrate on establishing our offense.

Of course, I was the first draft choice of the Cowboys that year—in reality, the Cowboys' first draft choice ever.

The Cowboys needed to put fans in the stands— especially if they were going to be competing against Lamar Hunt and his AFL Dallas Texans. Our offense wasn't exactly what one would call exciting to watch. Something needed to be done and done now!

As a defensive coach with the Giants, Tom had studied each and every offensive strategy of the other NFL teams. While with the Giants, he had devised the 4-3 defensive strategy.

In order for the 4-3 strategy to be effective, the defense must be able to recognize a formation, know the plays that can be run from that particular formation, and recognize certain keys that tell them which play or plays to expect. Decreasing the length of recognition time was imperative in beating an offense. The less time the defense had to recognize an offense, the harder it would be for them to stop it.

With that, Tom developed the multiple offense system. This system integrated every formation ever known. Here's how it worked. Prior to snapping the ball, the linemen would shift and the backfield would move. This allowed the offensive unit to run approximately 40 or 50 basic plays off eight or more different formations.

Before the multiple offensive system came into existence, there were only two basic offensive formations with only a couple of play options from each.

With the offense constantly in motion just before the snap of the ball, the defense didn't have time to recognize what offensive play was going to take place. You have to remember that back then our offensive line was extremely weak, so the more confusion that we could create for the defense, the more time the quarterback had to either pass or hand off the ball.

Our first game of the '61 season put us in the victory column. On a last-second field goal, we beat Pittsburgh 27–24. It was the Cowboys' first regular-season win. We enjoyed being 1–0 so much that we decided to make it 2–0 with a win over the Vikings. That day Don Perkins showed Coach Landry what he was really made of—that he was a great runner. That same year Perkins ran for over 800 yards. He finished second only to Bears tight end Mike Ditka for the Rookie of the Year Award.

Coach Landry liked to alternate his quarterbacks on every other play—first LeBaron and then Meredith, or vice versa. He wanted to utilize Eddie's experience while allowing Meredith to create his own.

The Cowboys ended their 1961 season with a 4–9–1 record—and two of those wins were against the expansion team, the Minnesota Vikings.

The 1962 season was an improvement from the previous season. We won several games with great offensive football. Coach was still alternating Don and Eddie in the games. The fans and the press made it very clear that they wanted the youthful Meredith to be their quarterback.

The Cowboys ended their 1961 season with a 4–10 record.

Coach was already aware of the fact that Meredith would be the starting quarterback and the future of the Cowboys, but he was afraid of destroying his confidence by rushing him into the position too quickly. Even though our offensive backfield was improving, the offensive line was still ineffective. And Don wouldn't stand a chance against a tough defensive line. They would physically destroy him—not to mention the mental anguish from the media and fans.

Being a Dallas Cowboys quarterback in those days was not considered a glamorous position. It required a strong survival instinct. Eddie LeBaron was a survivor, and in those early days he did something that I had never seen another quarterback do.

During one of our games, I noticed Eddie step up behind the center and then raise his hand prior to taking the snap. He did the same thing on the second down and then again on the third.

When he came off of the field, Coach asked him why he kept raising his hand before the snap. Eddie told him that he thought it might help if he signaled for a fair catch before the ball was snapped.

The stat totals for the '62 season showed some improvement. The offense scored more points than ever before, and our season record improved to 5–8–1.

But at team meetings Coach let the game films speak for themselves. Mistakes were many, and there was no "high" to be found in the highlights. Coach Landry was especially attuned to the number of "look out" plays in each series. A look out play is a play that's executed when the pass blocker fails to do his job, then yells to the quarterback, "Look out!"

Another costly blunder came in a game against Pittsburgh. The Cowboys had intercepted a Bobby Layne pass on our own 1-yard line. On first and ten, Eddie threw a bomb downfield to Frank Clarke, who ran 99 yards into the end zone for a Cowboys touchdown.

While we were celebrating on the sideline, we noticed that one of the officials had thrown a penalty flag back at the goal line of the Cowboys. It turned out that the Steelers' 6′6″, 280-pound defensive tackle, "Big Daddy" Lipscomb, had been held by one of our lineman. Now here's where it gets crazy. According to the referee, the infraction occurred two yards deep in *our* end zone. Upon motioning the play back, the ref signaled a safety to Pittsburgh!

Coach went ballistic! He charged onto the field and got right into the referee's face. Landry protested the call and demanded an explanation from the officials. Here's what the rule stated: an offensive penalty occurring in the offensive team's end zone will result in an automatic safety.

Coach became even more upset. He continued shouting at the ref and at the other officials, declaring that he had never heard of such a ridiculous rule.

Of course, the officials agreed with the referee, and Landry stormed off the field. But before reaching the sideline, he turned to the ref and said, "You better be right! That's all I can say. You better be right!"

Upon checking the *Official Rules of Professional Football*, it turned out that the official was right. And to add insult to injury, the Steelers beat us by a score of 30–28—a two-point differential.

Finally, the fans had become a part of the game!

But one good thing came out of the whole mess. Throughout all the screaming, protesting, and confusion that was happening on the field, the crowd got involved and booed the ref's call for 10 straight minutes. Finally, the fans had become a part of the game!

All in all, it seemed that fate, not to mention the rulebook, was against us. But in reality we were our own worst enemy. For instance, when we were playing the Browns Meredith decided to call a last-minute audible at the line of scrimmage. Both of our guards—6′1″, 243-pound Joe Bob Isbell and 6′1″, 243-pound Andy Cvercko—read the play wrong.

Joe Bob thought his job was to pull and trap, while Andy thought he was to pull. On the snap, both men pulled, ran in opposite directions, and smashed into each other behind the center. Now, mind you, this was in front of 80,000 screaming fans. It was even better when we saw it on game film the following day. I thought the guys were going to fall off their chairs laughing.

Another folly occurred one day during practice. Meredith threw a pass that was intercepted by Cornell Green. I don't know what got into Don, but he chased Cornell up and down the field while at the same time brandishing his helmet about as if it were a weapon. Once again the team cracked up with laughter watching the films. In both cases, Coach didn't seem to find any humor in them. At our next team meeting, he stood in front of us with that stoic, stony face and said, "Gentlemen, nothing funny ever happens on a football field—if we can help it."

Coach expected his players to become his definition of what a professional football player should be. A player should have his standards set high, he should be serious about his performance both on and off the field, and he should be proud of the results. Coach Landry posted a quote from Vince Lombardi in the locker room that defined this philosophy: "The quality of a man's life is in direct proportion to his commitment to excellence."

Coach Landry always surrounded himself with players and staff who were self-motivated and enthusiastic about meeting his expectations—in other words, keeping Coach happy. But when a player performed poorly on the field, he wouldn't say a word. He would just give you that look of total disgust—otherwise known as "the look."

You *never* wanted get the look, because it meant that you were responsible for creating a major screwup. Physical mistakes were much more acceptable to Coach than mental mistakes.

You never wanted get the look, because it meant that you were responsible for creating a major screwup.

If you were one of those who was unfortunate enough to have experienced the look more than a few times, most likely you wouldn't be a Cowboy much longer.

Coach's priorities in life were God, family, and football. His priorities were for real, and he truly believed in them. He was the man in the fedora and tie, the man who felt obliged to communicate a sense of morality in what he perceived as being "immoral times."

He never smoked or swore and drank wine only if he was at a function in the home of Cowboys owner Clint Murchison.

As constant as his beliefs, Tom was unemotional at meetings, practices, or games. He spoke in the same voice whether he was happy, sad, or angry. Players like Pete Gent, Bob Hayes, and Duane Thomas thought he was distant and robotic. In the beginning, Thomas "Hollywood" Henderson found him to be cold, stoic, and unreachable. He later learned to love and admire Tom.

Coach has the reputation of a man who lacks emotion and feeling. That isn't so. His sideline demeanor was his way of focusing on the game. He felt that a show of emotion interfered with his ability see things clearly.

Coach never lost confidence in his team or his system. He continued to let the team know that they were improving and with time, experience, and the right players, they would become winners. After all, our team record improved from 0–11–1 in 1960 to 4–9–1 in 1961 and to 5–8–1 in 1962.

The 1963 season was full of anticipation and desire. We finally settled in at our training camp at California Lutheran College in Thousand Oaks, California. The Cowboys would return every summer for the remainder of my career with the team.

At Cal Lutheran there were two practices a day—one at 9:00 AM and the other at 3:00 PM. Our schedule was rigidly controlled. There were only three things that thrilled us during the drudgery of training camp. They were breakfast (7:00 AM to 8:00 AM), lunch (12:00 PM to 1:00 PM), and dinner (6:00 PM to 7:00 PM). During dinner the rookies had to entertain the veterans by singing their school songs and other popular requests. After dinner there would be a meeting that would run from 7:30 to 9:30 or 10:00. We had Wednesday and Saturday evenings off with curfews of 11:00 PM. Of course if we were late to any of the above we were automatically fined.

The mountainous terrain surrounding the college was beautiful. Every day in the late afternoon we would jog over the mountains. Behind them stood a large ranch that was home to many movie sets. As a matter of fact, the TV series *Gunsmoke* was filmed there as well as the reenactment of the historic flag raising on Iwo Jima.

One day while reviewing game film during a team meeting, I had a revelation. I noticed that each time the ball was snapped or I made contact with my opponent, I blinked. Blinking causes the loss of approximately a millisecond—which may not seem like a lot, but in football it could mean the difference between getting the advantage over your opponent or allowing him to get the advantage over you.

So when attending practice or meetings, I would gently touch my eyeballs over and over until I got to the point where I would no longer blink. The players used to make fun of me, but before long they were doing it too.

While in my stance as a lineman, I would concentrate on my opponent so intensely that I could clearly see every whisker on his face. At the same time I would be watching the ball. At the moment the ball was snapped, I would tackle the opposition and, without blinking an eye, would be able to see which direction he was attempting to go.

It was about this time that we were beginning to see a major improvement in the defense. Players such as 6′6″, 250-pound end George Andrie; Jerry Tubbs; Chuck Howley; 6′3″, 208-pound back Cornell Green; and myself had become the core players of this unit. That year we added 6′1″, 221-pound Alabama linebacker Lee Roy Jordan.

I would gently touch my eyeballs over and over until I got to the point where I would no longer blink.

The Cowboys were even favored to win the Eastern Conference that year. Another plus was that owner Lamar Hunt and his AFL team, the Dallas Texans, had relocated their franchise to Kansas City, where they were now known as the Kansas City Chiefs. This meant that the fans whose loyalty was once devoted to the Texans would change sides and cross over to the NFL's Dallas team. We really started to believe that this was going to be our year.

Meredith had taken over for LeBaron at the quarterback position. I had a great deal of confidence that Don would take the team in the right direction. He really looked good. When we played the 49ers at Kezar Stadium, Meredith threw for a total of 460 yards. He had a great rhythm going.

After beating San Francisco we went on to play the Philadelphia Eagles, and we were once again victorious. Don was at the top of his game. We began to envision our team as a future contender. But once again, it was not meant to be.

9

Tragedy Strikes

THE 1963 SEASON SAW THE COWBOYS in the win column only four times. Both the offense and defense struggled, and both were challenged by far-superior teams.

But on a brisk November day in Dallas, the nation's impression of the Lone Star State and all those it encompassed would be forever tarnished, and the Cowboys would soon find themselves to be considered indirectly responsible for a tragedy.

Our Friday afternoon practice on November 22, 1963, was like that of any other Friday. Our next road trip would take us to play the Browns in Cleveland, and we were eager to be at the top of our game.

Shortly after we began our workout we saw one of our trainers running out on the field shouting. President John Kennedy and Texas governor John Connolly had been shot at 12:30 PM while riding in the presidential motorcade through Dealey Plaza in downtown Dallas. The incident took place only three miles away from our practice facility. To say that the team was stunned would be an understatement. At first we didn't believe what the trainer had said, but then reality set in.

Coach canceled practice, and everyone hurried home to listen to the radio or watch the televised broadcasts. At 1:00 PM the sad and somber voice of news reporter Walter Cronkite spoke those chilling words over the airwaves: "John Fitzgerald Kennedy, the 35th president of the United States, is dead."

The NFL decided not to cancel any of the games that were scheduled for the upcoming weekend. This turned out to be a big mistake. The city of Dallas and the state of Texas were criticized and blamed by the rest of the nation for the loss of its beloved president.

When we arrived in Cleveland to play the Browns, the baggage handlers at the airport and at the hotel refused to handle our luggage because we were from Dallas. We had to unload our own baggage from the plane and assist our trainers and equipment managers with tasks that were customarily taken care of by airport and hotel staff. We didn't venture far from the hotel or eat at any of the local restaurants. We basically stayed within the confines of the building. Workers and hotel staff, whom we normally would talk and joke with, were no longer speaking to us. Because our welfare and safety were at risk, we had to be escorted to the game by the local police.

Because our welfare and safety were at risk, we had to be escorted to the game by the local police.

Before the start of the game, a moment of silence was held in memory of President Kennedy. Once over, the announcer began to introduce the Cowboys' players. Immediately a wave of boos encompassed the stadium. We had never been confronted by anything like it before, and to tell you the truth, it was frightening. Don Meredith told the press, "Here we come out, the Dallas Cowboys, with our stars on our hats, and it was like going to the lions with the Christians."

We were genuinely worried about getting killed. We wondered if there were any snipers around the stadium. Throughout the game we wore our helmets and kept our capes on because some of the Cleveland fans threw bottles at us.

The Cowboys were perceived as conspirators in the president's assassination simply because we came from Dallas.

The Cowboys were perceived as conspirators in the president's assassination simply because we came from Dallas. From then on we were booed thunderously and frequently in every city of every team we played. The dissatisfaction and contempt for the team didn't end with the '63 season—it continued into the next.

We were even booed on our home field in Dallas—but for reasons other than the death of the president. The fans' love affair with the Dallas Cowboys was at an all-time low. They were sick and tired of watching us lose football games. Four years of losing seasons were enough. Something had to change, and soon.

Fingers began pointing at the coaching staff. There was talk that Coach would be fired. But on February 5, 1964, Clint Murchison Jr. shocked the football world by offering Coach Landry a 10-year contract extension. For a coach whose team record was 13–38–3, this proved to be an unparalleled show of support by management. Landry couldn't believe it, and neither could anyone else.

To the NFL, whose acronym has been said to mean "Not For Long" by former Houston and Atlanta coach Jerry Glanville, this was totally absurd. But Coach Landry always felt it was God's plan for him to coach, and Dallas was where he would implement that plan.

My dad and me. I was three years old. PHOTO COURTESY OF THE LILLY FAMILY

I probably had the best parents anyone could ask for. They encouraged me in all my endeavors and were my biggest fans. I'm proud of the Christian home they raised me in. PHOTO COURTESY OF THE LILLY FAMILY

Riding my bike at my grandmother's home in Throckmorton, Texas, in 1944. I was five years old. PHOTO COURTESY OF THE LILLY FAMILY

Pendleton High School All-Star Game in Portland, Oregon. I am No. 29. PHOTO COURTESY OF THE OREGONIAN

*At the Hula
Bowl my
senior year at
TCU.* PHOTO
COURTESY OF
TEXAS CHRISTIAN
UNIVERSITY

*My rookie season
with Dallas. Notice
all the holes in the
jersey from offensive
linemen's fingers.*
PHOTO COURTESY OF
THE DALLAS COWBOYS

Getting ready for practice in the training-camp locker room. Closest to the camera are Bob Hayes (left) and Larry Cole (right). PHOTO COURTESY OF BOB LILLY

Head coach Tom Landry was always like a father to me. He has forever impacted my life, and I am proud that I had the privilege of playing for him.
PHOTO COURTESY OF BOB LILLY

Defensive line coach Ernie Stautner was one of the toughest coaches I ever had the pleasure of working with. He was a great guy, and he gave us the benefit of his experience. He helped me a lot with some of my defensive moves, and he taught me how to head-butt.

Defensive secondary coach Dick Nolan and Coach Landry had ties from their Giants days together. Dick gained a good reputation as a coach and was responsible for implementing the flex defense.

Offensive backfield coach Ermal Allen joined the Cowboys' staff in 1962. His knowledge of football was infinite, and he was an excellent teacher of the game. PHOTO COURTESY OF BOB LILLY

I will never forget my first team meeting at training camp in Northfield, Minnesota. Coach Landry put God first, family second, and football third. I really thought that he had his priorities backward, but now I am convinced that he had them right all along. PHOTO COURTESY OF BOB LILLY

Dandy Don Meredith. If ever a nickname perfectly fit someone, it was Meredith's. He was our quarterback of the future—a guy with a great arm and a wonderful personality. Always laughing and clowning around, Don was the bright spot in the days when our teams performed so poorly. During practice he would come out of the huddle singing "I Didn't Know God Made Honky-Tonk Angels." Everyone would crack up...well, everyone except Coach Landry. PHOTO COURTESY OF BOB LILLY

Mike Gaechter was a sprinter at the University of Oregon and was later signed by the Cowboys as a free agent. Mike was extremely fast and went on to become a tough-hitting strong safety.
PHOTO COURTESY OF BOB LILLY

Lee Roy Jordan joined the Cowboys in 1963 and was a number one draft choice out of Alabama. As a middle linebacker, Lee Roy was intense, tough, and confident. He was a real asset to the Cowboys organization. PHOTO COURTESY OF BOB LILLY

Craig Morton was the Cowboys' number one draft pick in 1965. A graduate of Cal Berkeley, Morton came to the Cowboys as Don Meredith's understudy. He played a total of 18 years for the Cowboys, Giants, and Broncos. PHOTO COURTESY OF BOB LILLY

10

Improving the Team with Technology and the Flex

THE 1964 SEASON SAW THE DEPARTURE of Eddie LeBaron, who retired from the game in order to begin his law practice. The offense now belonged solely to Don Meredith.

Bad luck seemed to follow us into the new season. Don tore the cartilage in his knee during a preseason game but refused to turn over the reins to anyone else—besides, there wasn't anyone else. He courageously played out the entire season with the injury.

What made things even worse was that our offensive line couldn't protect him. It's true that we were better than before, but even a healthy quarterback would have trouble scrambling and dodging the defense, much less an injured one.

When it came to Don's performance on the field, the press was merciless. One sportswriter quipped, "Yardage lost attempting to live." The physical pain in itself was tough enough to bear. Don didn't need to endure the scrutiny of the media too.

Even though we won our last game of the '64 season, we still finished the year with a losing 5–8–1 record.

Computers were incorporated into the Dallas Cowboys' coaching and scouting staff in 1965. We needed a better, more efficient way to analyze new college talent because the previous methods were obviously not working.

Tex Schramm was a systematic organizer. From his network days at CBS, he had the opportunity to work with and learn about computers. Tex figured if they could compile, organize, and analyze data for the television networks, why couldn't they do it for football?

Collaborating with Tom and Gil Brandt, Tex contacted the Service Bureau Corporation (SBC), a subsidiary of IBM. In turn, SBC sent the Cowboys a computer genius from India by the name of Salam Querishi. But Salam knew nothing about American football, and the Cowboys' coaches and scouts knew nothing about computers.

They finally worked out the kinks in communication, and Salam was given the 300 variables for computer evaluation. In those days, computers could digest only eight variables at a time. The list needed to be refined.

Finally, after hundreds of hours of work, not to mention prototypes behind them, the team and the computer genius came up with five variables to be analyzed. They were character, competitiveness, strength and explosiveness, quickness and body control, and mental alertness.

Because the human factor can cause a bias in measuring quality, Salam created a questionnaire for each scout to use when evaluating the five variables. Assigned scores of 1–9 were given to each of the variables. Upon analyzing the data and allowing for degrees of freedom for bias, the system proved to be the key to our future success.

Because we began this process with the evaluation of college freshmen and then continued to follow their career throughout their remaining collegiate years, the organization didn't hesitate to spend a draft pick on a player who might not be available for another year or so.

In the 1964 draft, the Cowboys used six of their picks on future players. Three of those players were Bob Hayes, a 6′0″, 187-pound wide receiver out of Florida A&M; Roger Staubach, a 6′3″, 197-pound quarterback out of Annapolis; and Jerry Rhome, a 6′0″, 190-pound quarterback out of Tulsa.

Hayes was a world champion sprinter and was in the midst of training for the '64 Olympics. Quarterback Roger Staubach, who had just graduated from the Naval Academy, had to complete his four-year military commitment before playing for the Cowboys. Quarterback Jerry Rhome still had another year to fulfill at the University of Tulsa.

Gil Brandt and his scouts searched the entire nation to find talent from smaller academic institutions and predominantly black colleges. At a little-known college by the name of Elizabeth City State, Gil found a future Cowboy star in 6′6″, 260-pound defensive lineman Jethro Pugh.

Nondraftees included Pete Gent, a 6′4″, 205-pound basketball forward from Michigan State, and Cornell Green, an All-American hoops star from Utah State. Neither had played college football but each was a talented athlete, and Brandt knew he could find both of them a spot with the Cowboys. Next, Coach Landry came up with another one of his innovations: quality control. He explained it to the team like this:

Before you can assure the consistent quality of your product, you have to find where any problems are. I instituted the foundation of a quality control program at the end of our very first season in Dallas. We took all the game film for the season, cut it apart, and reassembled

> *it by specific plays—all the fullback draw plays together,
> all the screen passes, all the off-tackle slants—and put
> it in chronological order for the entire season. Then we
> could trace the effectiveness of a specific play throughout
> the season. We could see whether it became more or less
> objective, what changed, what needed to be changed to
> make it work better, and whether or not we should even
> keep it in the playbook for next year.*

Tom hired a quality-control coach, Ermal Allen, the 1947 quarterback and defensive back with the Cleveland Browns. Allen's only job was to splice and analyze game film, evaluate the effectiveness of each play, and chart the tendencies of the opposition for the Cowboys. This gave Tom the upper hand in preparing for future games because he knew what to expect from his opponent based on down and distance. Coach also changed the time line of evaluating the film from the end of the season to the end of each game.

At meetings he would effortlessly chart plays on the blackboard. He was one of the first coaches in football to chart opposing offensive patterns—studying exactly how many times a team ran to the right, to the left, and up the middle and knowing when they would do it again.

It didn't matter what kind of question you asked him because he always had an answer. He ran that football team like a business; the meeting room with a blackboard in it was his office. Though poised and dignified, he also had that impersonal side to him. He was really a coach's coach—not a player's coach. Discipline and consistency were his motivators.

The technology era was now in full swing. Even the job of our cameraman Bob Friedman had been enhanced. He not only filmed the entire game but was now filming our entire practices as well.

Coach's industrial engineering ideas didn't stop here. He hired Dr. Ray Fletcher, industrial psychologist, to help us more easily define our offensive and defensive philosophies plus establish realistic team and individual goals. It was devised to give everyone a sense of direction and, believe me, it worked.

The 1965 season saw an exceptional number of talented rookies during training camp at Cal Lutheran.

The 1965 season saw an exceptional number of talented rookies during training camp at Cal Lutheran. Coach Landry's number one draft choice was the 6′4″, 214-pound quarterback Craig Morton out of the University of California, Berkeley. Morton would be utilized as a backup to Meredith, who had endured a considerable number of injuries the previous year. Morton and former University of Tulsa quarterback Jerry Rhome both looked promising. Malcolm Walker, a 6′4″, 250-pound center from Rice; defensive tackle Jethro Pugh; and 6′6″, 265-pound lineman Ralph Neely from Oklahoma together enhanced the talent of the Cowboys.

Coach was particularly impressed with a free-agent quarterback out of South Carolina. Dan Reeves wasn't the most skilled player and certainly could not compete with Meredith, Morton, and Rhome, but his strong will and character is what most impressed Tom, so much so that Coach was determined to place him on the roster. He finally found a spot for him as a running back.

The final offensive weapon was Bob Hayes, otherwise known as "the World's Fastest Human." Watching him run a postpattern play was all it took to convince Coach of his tremendous speed and talent. There wasn't a defensive back in the league who could catch him—or, for that matter, even keep up with him.

In 1963 Coach shifted me from defensive end to the tackle position. It had taken me two seasons to mature and really learn and implement Tom's defensive strategy. He was extremely pleased with my dominance and performance on the field.

By 1964 the old 4-3 defense that Coach had developed while with the Giants way back when was now being utilized by many of the other NFL teams. Our defense was forced to readjust. That's when Tom redeveloped the scenario and named it the flex defense.

By 1965 the team had had a chance to study it for a year and now had a clear understanding of the system and how it worked.

Another factor that prompted Coach to change to the flex came in the form of coach Vince Lombardi. Although they were good friends off the field, on the field Lombardi was Landry's nemesis.

Vince had devised a Packers offense that was appropriately named "run to daylight" because there was always plenty of daylight to be found within the Dallas defense. So Coach Landry came up with a defensive strategy to darken that daylight.

Sportswriter Rick Gosselin of the *Dallas Morning News* gives perhaps the best description of the flex defense:

> *There are eight natural gaps along the line of scrimmage. Traditional defenses of the day asked the four linemen to control two gaps apiece. A defensive tackle, for instance, had to control the gaps between the center and guard and the guard and tackle. The premium was on power. Stymie the blocker, find the ball, then make the play.*
>
> *The flex gave Landry's defensive front a picket-fence look. The right end and left tackle lined up in conventional spots along the line of scrimmage, nose to nose*

with blockers. But the right tackle and left end lined up a few feet back of scrimmage, which afforded them better pursuit lanes laterally.

Next Landry asked his defenders up front to control one gap apiece, except for the middle linebacker. He had to control two, the gaps on either side of center.

The flex defense was a way of forcing the play back against itself—in other words, asking his linebackers and defensive backs to move the opposing players where they really didn't want to go. It revolutionized the defense and opened the door for all the variations of zones and man-to-man coverage. It also introduced motion offenses and made popular situational substitutions. It gave the Cowboys a chance at winning.

Our preseason games were difficult to analyze. We had finally beaten Lombardi's Packers, who, by the way, went on to become the 1965 NFL champions, but were badly defeated the following week by the Vikings by a score of 57–17.

Our final preseason game was played against the Bears in Tulsa. With Craig Morton showing difficulty adjusting to the complex offensive scheme, Coach rotated Meredith and Rhome at the quarterback position.

Rhome easily won the competition by connecting 10 out of 17 passes and throwing three touchdowns in an impressive Cowboys win. But Coach wasn't going to allow the press to have a field day over the probability of a quarterback controversy. It had already been decided—there wouldn't be one.

Tom would never forget how courageously Don played the year before. Through all the pain and hurt, he never gave up. It was only fair that Meredith be given the chance to prove what he could do while healthy and behind a more experienced offensive line.

The regular season had begun, and we won our first two home games—the first over the Giants and the second over the Redskins. Not only were we happy about our victories, but the administration was elated over the total paid attendance for both games. It computed to be more than the entire attendance of the Cowboy's inaugural year in 1960. The only person who wasn't excited about our conquests was Don Meredith.

He hadn't passed well in either of the two games and, to add insult to injury, we lost the next three games with Don at the helm. Finally, Coach began alternating Rhome and Craig Morton. Both rookies looked good, but Coach was determined to give Don his due by starting him in the next game against Pittsburgh. His justification for doing this was that the offensive unit needed an experienced leader, and he felt that Don was the one to do it. Besides, it wasn't too late in the season to take that chance.

The game against the Steelers was to be played in Pittsburgh. We knew we were the better team, but when the gun sounded and time had run out, we had lost 22–13. Don had completed only 12 of 34 passes for the day.

The atmosphere in the locker room after the game was one of disappointment and frustration. When Coach entered the room, no one looked up.

His voice cracked as tears streamed down his face.

Landry was searching for words when he finally said, "This is the first time I had been truly ashamed of our team's performance." Not a word was spoken by any of the players. The room had become deathly silent. Then Coach added, "I'm sorry. It's my fault."

His voice cracked as tears streamed down his face.

The team remained silent, all except Meredith, who, witnessing Coach's distress over the team's performance, said, "No, Coach. It's my fault."

Tom knew the press would be waiting outside the locker room, sharpening their claws in anticipation of the postgame interview. The big question was, who would be the starting quarterback next week?

Coach responded to the press by saying, "I haven't decided as yet. In the meantime, I will be reevaluating our quarterback situation." Then he abruptly ended that interview.

For the next two days Tom wrestled with trying to make the right decision. Should he go with two inexperienced quarterbacks, which would go against everything he believed in regarding playing a quarterback before his time? Or should he go with an experienced and seasoned Meredith, whose poor passing performance for the season totaled only 38 percent?

Two days later at the weekly noontime press conference Coach announced his decision. He would be counting on the experienced Meredith to do the job and help the Cowboys get back in the winning column.

With Tom's confidence in Don, the Cowboys went on to win five of the last seven games with a season record of 7–7. It was the first year the team broke even.

The Playoff Bowl
We ranked second in the Eastern Conference in 1965 behind the Browns and had achieved our first postseason appearance in the Playoff Bowl in Miami against the great Johnny Unitas and the Baltimore Colts.

The Playoff Bowl was a game played between the two conference runners-up. It was also referred to as the NFL's Losers' Bowl.

I don't know why it was called the Playoff Bowl, because when the game was over, win or lose, neither team advanced. It was the end of the season for both teams.

We weren't about to let the Colts upstage us, so some of our players signed Tex Schramm's name to our food and beverage charges!

When we arrived in Florida prior to game day, the Cowboys found out that the owner of the Baltimore Colts had not only allowed the players to bring their wives, but they had an open restaurant tab that they could use for food and drinks. All that was needed was their signatures.

The Colts owner also allowed his players a $20-a-day allowance while the Cowboys had a $12-a-day allowance. We weren't about to let the Colts upstage us, so some of our players signed Tex Schramm's name to our food and beverage charges!

When game day arrived, the Colts trounced us by a score of 35–3. Again, the press couldn't wait to get ahold of Coach so he could give them an explanation for the embarrassing loss. Tom's answer was short and concise: "It was a team effort." End of interview.

11

Post-Merger Successes

THE YEAR 1966 PROVED TO BE extremely innovative for pro football. On June 8, 1966, after years of bitter arguing and verbal battles, which included lawsuits, the NFL and the AFL announced their agreement to merge.

The Cowboys' Tex Schramm and Lamar Hunt, owner of the Kansas City Chiefs, sat down together with commissioner Pete Rozelle and agreed that professional football would benefit both financially and image-wise if the two leagues were to become one.

It was decided that the first competition between the two leagues would commence at the end of the 1966 season. The winner of the AFL and the winner of the NFL would meet in an annual postseason, winner-take-all challenge that Lamar Hunt appropriately had called the "Super Bowl."

But Tom's main worry was getting through the regular season. If there was to be a postseason for the Cowboys, he would worry about it when the time came. In the meantime, his only concern was to establish a winning pattern so his players could get the emotional sense of victory.

We were pretty lucky in the '66 draft. We picked up 6′3″, 245-pound offensive guard John Niland from Iowa; 6′4″,

260-pound defensive lineman Willie Townes from Tulsa; 6´1˝, 206-pound running back Les Shy from Long Beach State; and 6´0˝, 205-pound running back Walt Garrison from Oklahoma State. Coach felt that Walt would be a good backup to fullback Don Perkins.

Our first two preseason games saw us in the win column once again. We beat both the Rams and the 49ers on their own turf and then came back home to the Cotton Bowl to find that it had been sold out for our annual exhibition game against Green Bay. In front of a home-field crowd, the Cowboys ran over the Pack 21–3.

For the first time in Cowboys history, we had won all five of our preseason games. Amazing! What was even more amazing is that we would go on to win our first four games in the regular season. Upon flying home to Dallas after a victory in New York, we were greeted at the airport by over 10,000 Cowboys fans. We ended the season with a 10–3–1 record, clinching the Eastern Conference title. The image of the city began to change. We were no longer considered the city that killed JFK.

For the first time in Cowboys history, we had won all five of our preseason games.

We all began to think that our time had finally arrived. Don Meredith was awarded the Bert Bell trophy for league MVP, and All-Pro honors were given to Bob Hayes, Cornell Green, Chuck Howley, and myself. Coach Landry was named Coach of the Year.

I might also add that in 1966 the Cowboys set an all-time NFL record with 61 quarterback sacks, and we did it without a lot of blitzing!

On January 1, 1967, the Cowboys hosted the Packers for the NFL Championship Game. This Dallas team would be the youngest to ever play in an NFL title game.

Lady Luck seemed to be on the side of the Packers right from the start. Green Bay scored 14 points before the offense even had a chance to get onto the field—seven points from a Bart Starr touchdown pass and another seven from a fumble on the following kickoff that resulted in a TD.

We came back to tie the game at 14 but ended up losing 34–27. We did, however, give them a heck of a fight.

Green Bay won the NFL title, and on January 15, 1967, they went on to play the AFL champions, the Kansas City Chiefs, in Super Bowl I at the Los Angeles Memorial Coliseum—the first-ever AFL-NFL world championship game. The Packers scored three second-half touchdowns to beat the Chiefs 35–10. Bart Starr was named the first Super Bowl MVP in NFL history.

The 1967 season began with high hopes for the Cowboys, but being able to duplicate the success of the previous year was not easy. First of all, Meredith broke his nose, twisted his knee, and cracked two ribs. On top of it all, he ended up contracting pneumonia and was on the injured reserve list for a month. Don's backup, Craig Morton, became his replacement.

But despite numerous small setbacks, we were finally getting the respect we deserved simply because we had won the Eastern Conference the year before. The other teams in the league were now following our every move…some more than others.

Los Angeles Rams coach George Allen turned his team around in 1966 and ended up with a winning season. His next game was against the Cowboys, and George wasn't one to pull punches when it came to winning.

One day while the Cowboys were practicing, an unknown vehicle was seen parked outside the practice field. When the organization sent someone out to the parking lot, the driver sped away. Luckily for the Cowboys, they were able to write down the license plate number. The police traced the plate, and they found that the car had been leased to a Rams scout named Johnny Sanders.

Not only did George Allen denounce the accusation made by Schramm to Commissioner Rozelle, but he had the audacity to insist that the Cowboys had sent out their own scout, Bucko Kilroy, to spy on the Rams practice.

When asked how they knew this, Allen responded, "Someone in the Rams organization observed a man up in a tree overlooking our practice, but before anyone had a chance to interrogate him, he quickly descended down the tree and escaped the premises."

What got the Cowboys laughing was the fact that Frank Joseph "Bucko" Kilroy was a 300-pound former offensive and defensive lineman who played with the Eagles from 1943 to 1955. There was no way he could shimmy up and down anything—much less a tree—and get away on foot without anyone catching him!

Anyway, despite all the name-calling and accusations, the Rams beat us at home by a score of 36–13.

12

We Can Do Everything but Win the Big One

WE FINISHED UP THE 1967 SEASON 9–5 and won the now-called Capitol Division of the Eastern Conference. Dallas hosted the Browns in a playoff game in the Cotton Bowl on December 24, 1967. The Western Conference playoffs would see Vince Lombardi and his Packers play George Allen and his Rams. The victors of both conferences would play in the NFL championship game. Although the Baltimore Colts (11–1–2) had tied for the best record in the league, they lost the new division tie-breaker to the Los Angeles Rams and were excluded from the playoffs.

Don's performance in the playoffs was practically flawless. He completed 10 of his first 12 passes, and we ended up crushing the Browns 52–14. The fans were so impressed with his gridiron presentation that he received a thunderous standing ovation from the crowd.

The Packers had won their game against the Rams 28–7 at Milwaukee County Stadium, and they had home-field advantage in the championship game that season.

With the temperature in the teens, we arrived in Green Bay on Friday, December 29—two days before the game. As a whole, the team felt good about their chances of winning. I remember

Don Meredith cupping his hands and saying, "Easy money, baby. Easy money."

The following morning, Ralph Neely occupied himself by throwing snowballs while the rest of the team waited for the bus to take us to practice. The temperature was 18 degrees, the sun was shining, and Lambeau Field was in relatively good shape. Everyone's spirits were up.

But by Sunday morning, those high spirits had faded into a memory. Just to give you an example of how cold it was, I watched George Andrie throw a glass of water on a window. Before the water could stream to the bottom of the sill, it had frozen. The temperature had dropped to 13 below zero, not counting the windchill factor. It was at that moment that I realized that this gridiron battle would be determined by the survival of the fittest, and it would be that team who would emerge victorious.

When Meredith boarded the bus to the stadium, his happy-go-lucky personality was a little more serious than usual. He yelled, "Well, let's go get 'em!" Lee Roy Jordan was standing behind Don, and he just laughed. We all thought that this would somehow work itself out right.

Vince Lombardi had just paid $80,000 for Lambeau Field's brand-new underground heating system. We hoped that the temperature would remain about the same for game day, but on the morning of December 31, the thermometer at the stadium read 16 degrees below zero. Apparently the new heating system was not strong enough to hold back the icy, cold winds that left the field frozen and slippery. This game would later become known as the Ice Bowl.

The game was about to begin. The captains from both teams shook hands, the referee flipped the coin, and Dallas won the toss, electing to receive.

Green Bay took a 14–0 lead early in the second quarter. If it wasn't for our defense, the score would have still been 14–0 at the half, but George Andrie recovered a fumble and literally slid into the end zone for a touchdown. A second fumble was recovered just before the half, allowing for a Cowboys field goal, making the score 14–10.

As we walked off the field and entered the locker room, we were literally numb. We couldn't feel our feet or hands. Team doctor Martin Knight was afraid that frostbite would set in. At the end of the game, his hunch proved to be right.

> *As we walked off the field and entered the locker room, we were literally numb.*

The second half started with the temperature dropping to 20 below zero and the windchill to more than 40 below. The field had become an ice rink. The conditions had become unbearable.

Neither team scored in the third quarter.

On the first play of the fourth quarter, Dan Reeves faked a sweep and then threw a 50-yard TD pass to Lance Rentzel, providing the Cowboys with a 17–14 lead. But our lead quickly diminished in the final seconds of the game.

With 16 seconds to go, Packers quarterback Bart Starr called for a quarterback sneak from the 1-yard line. Desperately holding onto the ball, Starr blasted across the goal line—ending not only the game but the Cowboys' season as well. Final score: Dallas 17, Green Bay 21.

The Cowboys were now officially declared "next year's champions." No team ever wants to be called that. That's about as bad as being called bridesmaids, which, in reality, is exactly what we were.

For the second consecutive year, Green Bay made it to the final game of the season. On January 14, 1968, Super Bowl II was played in the warm, sunny climate of Miami, Florida.

Bart Starr and company's opponents that day were the Oakland Raiders of the AFL. Once again, Lombardi and his team were victorious, defeating the Raiders 33–14. With a repeat of the previous year's performance, Bart Starr was once again named MVP of the Super Bowl.

The rumors of Coach Lombardi's retirement at the conclusion of Super Bowl II proved to be true. He not only left the game victoriously, he was generally regarded as one of the greatest football minds the NFL had ever seen.

Our flight home to Dallas after the Ice Bowl was a somber one. Coach Landry told us that the world doesn't stop when you lose and that we must think about the good things that happened to us and to look ahead. He truly felt that the only way a person could really become strong is to have setbacks. We had had more than our share.

Meredith took the blame for the loss and spoke of retiring from the game. When we arrived in Dallas, the press was eagerly waiting for us.

Tom told the press, "It's most disappointing to have this happen twice in a row. I guess we can do everything except win the big one." No one disputed the statement—not even Coach Landry.

13

Our Season to Shine Becomes a Season of Sadness

THE 1968 TRAINING CAMP LOOKED PROMISING. The Cowboys had drafted well, acquiring Mike Clark, a 6'1", 205-pound kicker out of Texas A&M; Ron Widby, a 6'4", 210-pound punter out of Tennessee; Blaine Nye, a 6'4", 251-pound offensive guard out of Stanford; and Larry Cole, a 6'5", 252-pound defensive lineman out of Houston. Our 6'6", 255-pound tight end, Rayfield Wright, was moved to the tackle position.

Even though we looked great on the practice field, Coach Landry was still insecure about the psychological trauma that might have been lingering from the two championship losses to Green Bay.

The team was genuinely committed to themselves and to Coach. We proved this by winning our first six games of the season. Even though we once again lost to the Packers, we still went on to post a 12–2 record—our best season ever. Both Don Perkins and Don Meredith had great years—and yes, Meredith had decided not to retire. We were beginning to believe that 1968 would be our season to shine.

On December 21, 1968, the Cowboys were once again pitted against Cleveland in the divisional playoffs. This was the same team that we blew out of the Cotton Bowl the year before, 52–14. We had also beaten them earlier in the season by a score of 28–7. But this time we were playing them on their turf, on the frozen shores of Lake Erie where many teams before us had tried and failed.

Even though we were tied 10–10 at the half, both the offensive unit and Meredith himself were exhibiting a dismal gridiron performance. The second half was worse than the first. Don threw two back-to-back interceptions that resulted in 14 points for the Browns. Finally, Coach pulled Meredith out and replaced him with Morton.

Tex Schramm walked over to Meredith, put his arms around him, and began to cry.

Even though Craig was able to find the end zone one time in the final quarter, it was too little, too late. Cleveland won 31–20.

As the final seconds of the game wound down, Tex Schramm walked over to Meredith, put his arms around him, and began to cry. Don did the same. Don was so distraught that he boarded a flight to New York, opting not to return home with the team. It was probably a good decision on Don's part because once in the air, Tex Schramm stood up in frustration and proclaimed to everyone on board, "A whole year shot in two and a half hours!"

Coach Landry told the press at the postgame conference, "This is my most disappointing day as a coach."

The 1969 season began with a sense of doubt from both the fans and the press. A 6′4″, 227-pound running back from Yale by the name of Calvin Hill was the Cowboys' number one draft choice. Gil Brandt and his staff raved about the Ivy League running back and praised his athleticism and skill. Still, not too many people had heard of Calvin Hill.

The fans' and the media's disappointment over what they had considered to be a poor draft season became minimal in scope as compared to the announcement of Don Meredith's retirement.

Coach Landry took the news hard, but he knew that between the physical and psychological burdens that Don had endured over the past ten years and the family concerns that he had been facing, leaving football would be best for him.

A teary-eyed Meredith made his statement to the press on July 5, 1969—just weeks before training camp was to begin. At that conference he told the reporters that he had come to love this man they call Coach Landry. In return, Coach had this to say to the press about Don: "I firmly believe that my decision in 1965 to stick with Don was the most important decision made in this club's history and led directly to our conference championships in 1966 and 1967."

14

Quarterback Controversy and Changes Afoot

FROM THE ORGANIZATION'S POINT OF VIEW, Meredith's retirement couldn't have come at a worse time. Craig Morton had taken over the number one quarterback position, but Morton's backup, Jerry Rhome, had requested that he be traded. The only backup quarterback that remained was a 27-year-old rookie by the name of Roger Staubach.

When Roger came to the Cowboys, Coach Landry thought he had died and gone to heaven.

Roger had just completed four years of military duty with the navy, and it was uncertain if he could recapture the successful gridiron career he had had at Annapolis. Even though he had won the Heisman, it was still a question that remained in the back of everyone's mind.

While on leave and still serving his military obligation, Roger was able to attend the '67 and '68 training camps. Roger looked as good as he did when playing for Navy. He still had the moves and the arm.

When Roger came to the Cowboys, Coach Landry thought he had died and gone to heaven. Roger was everything Coach thought a quarterback should be. He was dedicated, a team leader, a good Christian, an ex-navy man, and a good family man.

But the problem Tom had was that he already had a great quarterback in Craig Morton, and Craig wasn't the kind of guy who would just sit back and let a guy like Roger take his place.

Craig was a product of the University of California at Berkeley. He was tremendously skilled and had a mind for football. He had all the qualities of a great quarterback—all except one.

Morton, like Meredith before him, was famous for his partying. His pursuit of fun, drink, and women was at the top of his priority list. But to Coach Landry, Morton, like Meredith, was at the opposite end of the morals spectrum.

Craig proved he was a great athlete. He could stay out all night and still make practice in the morning, not to mention being able to casually throw 70 yards as though it were 20. He truly was a phenom in his own right.

Staubach and Morton were not only opposites off the field, they were opposites on the field as well. Craig stayed in the pocket regardless of the situation. He was not one to be frightened into throwing the ball just because the pass rush was ready to jump down his throat. Roger, on the other hand, was a scrambler, and that caused Coach Landry to worry about him getting injured. But when necessary, Roger was out of the pocket like a shot, avoiding defensive players left and right. In fact, that's how he got the nickname Roger the Dodger.

Both were great in their own way, which sparked a quarterback controversy. The media, the fans, and even Coach Landry himself didn't know which quarterback to play. Even our offensive and defensive teams had different theories as to who should start. The offense thought that Craig was the better quarterback while the defense felt that Roger could make things happen. Staubach was only a rookie while Morton had already established himself as an All-Pro quarterback.

When the preseason came along, Craig Morton was the new starter at the quarterback position. Craig looked impressive, as did halfback Calvin Hill. Calvin's exhibition of talent made a believer out of the media—not to mention the fans. He became an overnight success with the Cowboy organization.

We were also able to acquire a great tight end in an off-season trade with the Philadelphia Eagles: Mike Ditka, a 6′3″, 228-pound All-Pro. After playing six years with the Chicago Bears, Mike informed Coach George Halas that he had considered taking his loyalty to the AFL. With that, Halas traded him to the Eagles where he spent two seasons before being shipped to the Cowboys in 1969.

When Mike showed up at the Cowboys facility, he was in pretty bad shape. His competitive nature forced him to build himself back up to the All-Pro player that he had been; he became a valuable asset to the offensive unit.

The regular season had finally begun, and we won our opener. Even though Craig had a separated shoulder and was in pain the majority of the season, he proved to himself, to Coach, and to the team that he could get the job done.

Calvin Hill not only broke the Cowboys' single-game rushing record with 138 yards but tied All-Pro Jim Brown's all-time rookie rushing total of 942 yards. Not bad for a guy from an Ivy League school!

We finished the season with an 11–2–1 record and were once again divisional winners. In the Eastern Conference championship, we repeated our rivalry with the Cleveland Browns, but this time at the Cotton Bowl. As Yogi Berra would say, "It was déjà vu all over again."

In the first half of the game, Morton completed only three passes while Walt Garrison and Calvin Hill together posted a pathetic total of only 22 yards in seven carries. The score at the end of the first half was 17–0.

We came back onto the field with hopes high, but again our performance was low. By the fourth quarter the score was 31–7. To make matters worse, Morton threw an interception and the Browns ran it back for an 88-yard touchdown. On the next offensive play, Coach sent in Roger Staubach. He passed for one touchdown, but again it was too little, too late. Final score: Browns 38, Dallas 14.

In Super Bowl IV, Lamar Hunt and his Kansas City Chiefs defeated the Minnesota Vikings 23–7. The Dallas press immediately proclaimed, "It looked like the wrong team had left town." Over the past three years, and with the exception of the Baltimore Colts, the Cowboys' record exceeded that of any other in the NFL. But the fact remained that we never made it to the big one. By this time the press was perpetually referring to us as "next year's team."

Coach Landry once told our team, "The toughest championship to win is the first one. Once you do win, you have the psychological advantage of knowing you can. It gives you confidence. That's how success breeds success."

But what Coach didn't tell us was that failure will breed failure. He was convinced that the problem with the Cowboys was psychological, and he prepared to fight that problem.

A survey was handed out to everyone on the team. We were given strict instructions not to sign it so the results could remain anonymous. We were asked to evaluate the organization, the coaching staff, the offense and the defense, the training program, game plans, team discipline, spirit and commitment, mental toughness, and more.

After all the data had been collected, compiled, and evaluated by Coach Landry, his staff, and the Cowboys organization, things began to change. Beginning with our training program, Coach brought in a former Olympic weightlifting coach by the name of Alvin Roy.

Roy was considered to be a pioneer in the field of strength development and strength coaching. He created strength and weight training programs for many of the major college football teams and U.S. Olympic teams and later worked as a trainer coach for the NFL.

Before 1960, weight lifting was considered not only dangerous but detrimental to athletes—especially those involved in professional football. In 1963, Sid Gillman, coach of the San Diego Chargers, hired Roy as the league's first strength and conditioning coach. That same year the Chargers won the AFL championship with a 51–10 victory over Boston.

Communication between players and coaches also seemed to be a factor. Coach Landry revised coaching assignments and selected 26-year-old Dan Reeves to be the player/coach for the backfield. Dan may have been young, but he had both great character and an intellectual mind for the game.

Another change that was quickly noted by all was the letter we received just prior to training camp. Due to the individual performance standards created for each player, no one, including the starters, would be assured of job security until each of them had met those standards.

15

Duane Thomas Makes the Scene

THE 1970 DRAFT SEASON WAS A GOOD ONE. Former 49ers coach Red Hickey was now a scout for Coach Landry. Hickey was eager to draft this incredibly fast, 6′2″, 220-pound back out of West Texas A&M named Duane Thomas. Red called him the "best running back in the country without exception." Red thought Duane was better than halfback Calvin Hill, who had won Rookie of the Year honors the year before.

The Cowboys' computerized ranking system had rated him highly, but there was one problem—one serious problem—his attitude. This would later become an issue in his career.

When the Cowboys' turn to pick finally came around, Thomas was still available and was chosen in the first round. In addition to Duane Thomas, Coach added 6′1″, 193-pound defensive back Charlie Waters out of Clemson; 5′10″, 188-pound defensive back Mark Washington out of Morgan State; 6′3″, 255-pound offensive lineman John Fitzgerald out of Boston College; 6′5″, 247-pound defensive lineman Pat Toomay out of Vanderbilt; 6′1″, 220-pound linebacker Steve Kiner out of Tennessee; 6′0″, 193-pound running back Joe Williams out of Wyoming; 5′11″, 185-pound defensive back Pete Athas out of Tennessee; traded for 6′0″, 205-pound All-Pro cornerback Herb Adderley from the Green

Bay Packers; and signed a virtually unknown 6′0″, 168-pound safety and free agent from Ouachita Baptist College by the name of Cliff Harris. Cliff was so good and so tough that he made the team and became a starter by the time the regular season began.

But more than anyone else, Roger Staubach wanted to play Cowboys football. At one of our meetings Coach said, "There wasn't a quarterback in the league who'd ever won a championship with less than three years of experience."

With that statement, Staubach went nuts. He stood up and looked directly at Coach and said, "How can you judge every individual by the same yardstick? If you do that, I don't have a chance to start because I'm only in my second year. You've got to judge every individual separately!"

I think Coach Landry was a little shocked by his reaction. He tried to explain his philosophy to Staubach, but the quarterback wasn't buying it. His response to Coach was simply, "I feel I can physically make up for any mental shortcomings!"

Ironically, Craig Morton's shoulder surgery hadn't healed as quickly as the organization would have liked. Coach had no choice but to go with Roger for the first two games of the season. Although Dallas beat both Philadelphia and New York, Staubach's performance didn't really impress Coach Landry. Craig was ready to return to action by the third game. With Morton at the helm, we went on to lose to the Cardinals, Vikings, and Giants.

With a 2–3 record, we faced the St. Louis Cardinals at home. The Cardinals had a one-game lead on us, and it was imperative that we play well in front of a national audience. Did I mention that it was a *Monday Night Football* game?

When the gun sounded to end the game, we were defeated for a second time by St. Louis that year. We were not only defeated, we were disgraced. The final score was 38–0. We looked so bad that the crowd started chanting, "We want Meredith! We want Meredith!" I can only imagine what Don was thinking while sitting up in that booth with broadcasting partners Keith Jackson and Howard Cosell.

In the locker room Coach told us, "Maybe it was my fault, I don't know; but it was the worst performance of a Cowboys team I've ever seen." With our record at 2–4, I thought the Cowboys' season was all but over.

At practice the following day, Coach had come up with a different strategy. Since the other strategies were definitely not working, he decided that the best thing for the team to do was to relax, enjoy the rest of the season, and have fun. That same day we played a game of touch football and had a great time. The following week we beat the Washington Redskins 45–21. We stopped worrying and began enjoying the game.

> *That same day we played a game of touch football and had a great time.*

We won our next four games, which included the Packers, the Redskins at home in Dallas, the Browns, and the Oilers to clinch the NFL East title. Then we beat Detroit 5–0 in the divisional round of the playoffs. In the NFL Championship Game, we beat former Dallas assistant coach Dick Nolan and his San Francisco 49ers by a score of 17–10. Next stop: Super Bowl V.

Super Bowl V

Super Bowl V was played on January 17, 1971, on a clear, warm, 70-degree day at the Orange Bowl in Miami, Florida. It was the first championship game ever to be played on artificial turf.

The Cowboys walked onto the field confident and, most of all, ready to win. We were favored by two points.

Dallas took an early 6–0 lead with two field goals by Mike Clark. Several plays later, Colts quarterback Johnny Unitas threw a pass that bounced off the hands of Eddie Hinton and into the hands of Colts tight end John Mackey, who ran the ball 75 yards for six points.

Dallas took a 13–6 lead in the second quarter after Craig threw a seven-yard pass to Duane Thomas. A few plays later, Unitas was knocked out on a play and replaced by Earl Morrall.

In the fourth quarter, Morton was intercepted by Rick Volk; two plays later, Tom Nowatazke scored on a two-yard touchdown run. Jim O'Brien's PAT tied the game at 13–13.

With only a minute or so left in the game, Morton threw a pass that went through the hands of Dan Reeves and into the hands of Colts linebacker Mike Curtis. Two plays later and with five seconds left in the game, O'Brien kicked the game-winning field goal. Final score: Baltimore 16, Dallas 13.

At that very moment, my frustration had reached its peak. I ripped off my helmet and hurled it 58 yards into the air. I was just so disgusted with the way we had played, and to lose in the final seconds was the straw that broke the camel's back. I just lost it. What made matters even worse is that a rookie from the Colts brought my helmet back to me and said, "Mr. Lilly, here's your helmet." I felt about an inch tall.

Super Bowl V is also known as the Blunder Bowl because of the poor style of play, penalties, turnovers, and officiating mistakes. Both the Cowboys and the Colts scored a Super Bowl record of 11 combined turnovers in the game—seven for Baltimore and four by the Cowboys. Dallas also set an embarrassing Super Bowl record for penalties with 10, for a combined total of 133 yards lost.

The only high point of the game was when our linebacker Chuck Howley was awarded the MVP of the game. It was the first time in Super Bowl history that the award was given to a member of the losing team. It was also the first time that the quarterback didn't win the award.

On the other hand, the press ripped the team apart by referring to us as "next year's champions" and "bridesmaids of the NFL." That's something that no NFL team ever wants to hear.

1971

Even though we had moved out of the Cotton Bowl and into the new Texas Stadium in Irving, the beginning of the 1971 season didn't quite go as Coach had expected it would.

The press ripped the team apart by referring to us as "next year's champions" and "bridesmaids of the NFL."

But the fact that Morton was still having problems with his throwing arm paled in comparison to what Duane Thomas was doing to the Dallas Cowboys.

Duane had had a great rookie year and was ready to renegotiate his Cowboys contract, but his nonconformist attitude and disposition caused a lot of controversy within the organization. Tex Schramm adamantly refused to renegotiate Thomas's contract, and Duane stormed out of his office. Then he didn't show up for the first week of training camp in Thousand Oaks, California.

During the second week of camp, Duane not only had the audacity to show up a week late, but he brought along a friend that he insisted be given a tryout with the team. When Coach refused, Thomas again left the scene.

By this time Duane Thomas was enraged with the treatment he had received from the Cowboys. He immediately contacted the media and held a press conference in Dallas. There, he told the press that first, he was demanding a larger salary. He told them that the Cowboys had never gotten to the Super Bowl until he joined the team and wouldn't do it again if he didn't play. He also accused the Dallas organization of "mistreatment solely because [he was] black."

Next he began to verbally attack the coaches and the administration. He called Coach Landry "a plastic man who was actually no man at all." He said that Gil Brandt was a liar and Tex Schramm was "sick, demented, and completely dishonest."

Coach showed his usual calm and collected demeanor by responding to the press with, "Everyone is entitled to his own opinion."

Weeks at training camp had passed, and still no Duane. Coach had finally had enough and worked out a trade with New England for running back Carl Garrett and a future number one draft pick. Regardless of one person's talent, you sometimes have to go with what's best for the team, and getting rid of Thomas at that time was what was best for all.

When Duane arrived at New England he started right where he left off. As part of each NFL team physical, it is required that every player take a blood test and urinalysis prior to the beginning of each season. Duane refused to do so. Somehow he was still allowed to participate in training camp—but not for long. One of the Patriots coaches suggested that Thomas change his stance to enhance his performance. Once again, Duane refused and left camp—permanently. The Patriots immediately, if not sooner, invalidated the trade. Not only did we have to take Thomas back, but we had to give up Carl Garrett and the next year's number one draft pick. It wasn't a happy day for the Cowboys' organization.

Thomas refused to return to the Dallas team. By this time, Coach was more interested in working with Craig and Roger. Besides, he still had Calvin Hill. Both quarterbacks looked equally good, so Coach Landry decided to alternate them from one game to another.

Despite the fact that we entered the season with the reputation of not being able to win the big one, we started off the '71 schedule by winning our first two games, first against Buffalo 49–37, and then against Philadelphia 42–7. With Staubach knocked unconscious in the second game, it was up to Craig to start against Washington. Unfortunately, we lost the game 20–16. But regardless of the standings, I knew it always troubled Coach Landry to lose to his nemesis, Coach Allen.

In the fourth week of practice, Duane Thomas had decided to once again grace our team with his presence. And again, Coach Landry took him in.

While playing the Giants at home, Calvin Hill was injured and Coach had to send in Thomas. He ran nine times for a total of 60 yards.

Roger Staubach put pressure on Coach Landry as well—but it was different from what Duane was doing. Coach had replaced Staubach with Morton after a 13–6 lead at the half. Craig ended up finishing and ultimately losing the game. Roger was so angered by Coach's decision that he verbally voiced his disgust after the game. Roger's disappointment was due to the fact that he *wanted* to play and wanted Coach to give him that chance to prove himself. The quarterback controversy was still on.

On the other hand, Duane absolutely *refused* to talk to the media (not to mention his teammates), *refused* to wear a coat and tie on road trips, *refused* to answer at roll call, *refused* to open his playbook at team meetings, refused to do warmups with the team, and basically *refused* to cooperate with the coaches and the rest of the organization. His radical mood swings and disruptive behavior were beyond anything Coach Landry had ever seen before.

His radical mood swings and disruptive behavior were beyond anything Coach Landry had ever seen before.

Some of the players felt that Coach had a double standard when it came to Thomas. I think that the sole reason for the team's tolerance of Thomas was because of his athleticism and skill on game day.

Even though Coach Landry didn't care for the media's inferences regarding a quarterback controversy, he couldn't ignore this statement that Don Meredith made during a Monday night game:

> *It's Landry's responsibility as a head coach to pick a quarterback. Now after all this time, if he still has no idea which one is the best, then get another coach. I'm somewhat disappointed, but I'm sure not nearly as disappointed as Morton and Staubach, not to mention the other 38 players who are involved in this wishy-washy decision.*

Finally, after losing 23–19 to the Bears in Chicago, Coach made the decision to go with Roger. From that day on, we didn't lose another game the rest of the season. And to add icing to the cake, we shut out George Allen and his Redskins on their own turf by a score of 13–0. Coach Landry couldn't have been happier.

At the end of the Cowboys' regular season, Roger's stats proved why he was named the NFL's top-rated passer: 1,882 yards passing, 15 touchdowns, 343 yards rushing, and two touchdowns. He carried the ball 41 times and only threw four interceptions throughout the entire regular season.

Running backs Walt Garrison, Calvin Hill, and Duane Thomas also had outstanding seasons, as did wide receivers Lance Alworth and Bob Hayes. The backs rushed for a combined total of 1,690 yards and 20 touchdowns, and the receivers caught a combined total of 69 passes for 1,327 yards and 10 touchdowns.

Offensive linemen Forrest Gregg, Ralph Neely, John Niland, and Rayfield Wright were outstanding and contributed immensely to the Cowboys' success.

Our Doomsday Defense had given up only one touchdown in the last 18 quarters of the regular season and postseason. Linebackers Chuck Howley, Dave Edwards, and Lee Roy Jordan had a combined total of nine interceptions. Howley led the group with a total of five.

Defensive backs Herb Adderley and Mel Renfro and safeties Cliff Harris and Cornell Green had a combined total of 14 interceptions. Adderley led with a total of six.

We finished the regular season with an 11–3 record. In the playoffs we convincingly beat the Minnesota Vikings 20–12 and took care of the 49ers with a score of 14–3, allowing us to win the NFC title and a return trip to the Super Bowl.

16

Winning the Big One

ON JANUARY 16, 1972, IN FRONT OF A CROWD of 81,023 scream-ing fans at Tulane Stadium in New Orleans, Louisiana, the Dallas Cowboys took the field. Super Bowl VI was played on a sunny yet brisk day with the temperature holding at 39 degrees. We were favored by six points.

Miami won the toss and elected to receive, but we scored first after Larry Czonka fumbled and Chuck Howley recovered the ball. Several plays later, Mike Clark kicked a nine-yard field goal to give us a 3–0 lead.

On the Dolphins' second possession, I sacked Bob Griese for a 29-yard loss. On their next possession, Garo Yepremian missed a 49-yard field-goal attempt.

Later in the second quarter, Roger threw a seven-yard TD pass to Lance Alworth, making the score 10–0. With only seconds remaining in the first half, Yepremian kicked a 31-yard field goal making the score 10–3 and cutting our lead to seven.

We dominated the second half of the game. A pitchout from Roger to Duane Thomas on a three-yard sweep gave the Cowboys a 17–3 lead.

Our defensive unit was so pumped up that we didn't allow Miami to make even one first down the entire third quarter.

In the fourth quarter with only 12 minutes left to play in the game, Chuck Howley intercepted a Griese pass, and three plays later, Roger threw a seven-yard TD pass to tight end Mike Ditka, making the score 24–3.

The gun sounded, ending the game. We had finally won the big one. No longer would we be called "next year's champions." We were the Super Bowl champions—the best of the best in the NFL. The reality of establishing ourselves as America's Team had finally arrived.

As we carried Coach Landry off the field on our shoulders, his stone-faced demeanor had transformed into an exhilarating expression of joy and delight.

We had finally won the big one.

The celebration of champagne corks popping and the whooping and hollering from the team could be heard throughout the locker room. Owner Clint Murchison Jr. smiled and announced to the team, "This is a very successful culmination of our 12-year plan."

The climactic ending to it all was when Coach Landry was awarded the championship trophy by commissioner Pete Rozelle. Shortly after, Coach received a congratulatory call from President Nixon.

It was the first time I saw Coach really smile. In fact, he smiled for many days to follow.

The Super Bowl title validated the players, our coach, and our team and earned us a place among the NFL's elite teams. It not only rid the Cowboys organization of the criticism and pressure that had built up throughout the years, but it bestowed celebrity status on those involved. Players like Tony Dorsett, Cliff Harris, Thomas "Hollywood" Henderson, Ed "Too Tall" Jones, Lee Roy Jordan, Harvey Martin, Drew Pearson, Mel Renfro, Roger Staubach, Duane Thomas, Randy White, and Rayfield Wright would all see their stars rise in the decade of the '70s.

Seasons of Positive Change

The 1972 season started off on a bad note. Duane Thomas didn't show up for training camp until the fourth day. Once again, Coach had one of his talks with him, but this time he let Duane know that there would be only one set of rules, and they would apply to everyone…including him.

For the first few weeks, Duane went along with the program but still continued to ignore his teammates and eat by himself in his room. The final straw came when Thomas out-and-out refused to attend team meetings and practice. He said he "just didn't feel like going."

That did it for Coach. He immediately got on the phone and arranged a guaranteed trade with the Chargers, sending Thomas to San Diego. In return, the Cowboys acquired 6′2″, 210-pound running back Mike Montgomery and 6′1″, 185-pound wide receiver Billy Parks.

To make matters even worse, Roger Staubach separated his shoulder before the regular season even began. It was decided that the operation couldn't wait till the off-season, making Craig Morton our starting quarterback for the year.

All in all it really wasn't a bad season. We ended up with a 10–4 record, losing only to the Packers, the Redskins, the 49ers, and the New York Giants.

In the playoffs, we barely beat the 49ers in San Francisco by a score of 30–28. Late in the third quarter we were behind by 15 points. Coach took Morton out and replaced him with Roger, whose shoulder had healed well enough for him to play if needed.

Roger was a little rusty in the beginning, but by the fourth quarter—with 1:53 left in the game—Staubach came to life. With 1:30 left, Roger threw to Billy Parks for a touchdown, making the score 28–23 and putting the Cowboys within five points.

An onside kick was imminent. Our kicker, Toni Fritsch, kicked the ball sideways, and when 49er receiver Preston Riley tried to grab it, he was immediately hit by our rookie Ralph Coleman. The ball flew loose, and Mel Renfro recovered on the 50.

Within two plays we had taken the ball down to the 10-yard line. On the next play and with time running out, Roger threw a soft pass to Ron Sellers for the winning touchdown. Roger had done the impossible…he scored two touchdowns in the final minute and a half of the game.

Sadly enough, though, the following week we lost the NFC Championship Game to George Allen and his Washington Redskins by a score of 26–3. But all in all, it was a respectable year.

In 1973 the organization saw a drastic change in player personnel. Lance Alworth, George Andrie, Chuck Howley, and Mike Ditka all retired. In the '72 draft we acquired 5′10″, 209-pound running back Robert Newhouse out of Houston and Jean Fugett, a 6′3″, 225-pound tight end out of Amherst.

The rookies from our '73 draft included a 6′4″, 225-pound tight end out of Michigan State named Billy Joe DuPree; 6′5″, 260-pound defensive lineman Harvey Martin out of Texas A&M–Commerce; 6′1″,181-pound wide receiver Golden Richards out of Hawaii; and a virtually unknown 6′0″, 184-pound wide receiver out of Tulsa named Drew Pearson signed as an undrafted free agent.

Coach finally settled the quarterback controversy with the team, the media, and the fans by choosing Roger as his starter. Staubach once again showed his greatness on the field. He led the league in passing for the second time since the '71 season and guided the team to another 10–4 season and a berth in the divisional playoffs. Our four regular-season losses were to Washington, Los Angeles, Philadelphia, and Miami.

On December 23, 1973, in our playoff game at Texas Stadium, we convincingly beat the Rams 27–16. The highlight of that game was when Roger threw a short pass over the middle to Drew Pearson, who ran untouched for an 83-yard touchdown that sealed the game for Dallas.

Coach finally settled the quarterback controversy with the team, the media, and the fans by choosing Roger as his starter.

In the conference championship against Fran Tarkenton and the Vikings, we weren't as lucky. The Minnesota defense forced Roger to throw four interceptions and caused the Cowboys to fumble twice. Both Calvin Hill and I were unable to play in the game because of injuries. It was the only game I missed during my career. Walt Garrison played all day with a broken clavicle. The final score was Minnesota 27, Dallas 10.

The Vikings went on to play the Miami Dolphins on January 13, 1974, in Super Bowl VIII. Miami dominated the game and won by a score of 24–7. To this day, Minnesota has yet to win a Super Bowl.

The 1974 season began with a players' strike that kept the veteran players out of training camp until August 14. Calvin Hill announced to the organization that the '74 season would be his last as a Dallas Cowboy. He had just signed a contract to play for the new World Football League beginning in 1975. At his own request, quarterback Craig Morton was traded to the New York Giants.

But there were two bright spots in the '74 draft. The Cowboys' first pick in the first round was 6′9″, 271-pound defensive end Ed "Too Tall" Jones out of Tennessee State, and our third-round pick was 6′2″, 193-pound quarterback and punter Danny White out of Arizona State.

The one highlight of the season came on November 28, 1974. It was on Thanksgiving Day, and it was a nationally televised game against George Allen and his Washington Redskins.

With 10 minutes remaining in the third quarter and Washington leading 16–3, Redskins linebacker Dave Robinson tackled Staubach so hard that he knocked Roger out of the game. With Craig Morton gone, our only backup quarterback was rookie Clint Longley.

With very little experience, and unable to read the Redskins' defense, Clint figured that all he could do was scan the field, look for an open man, and throw the ball. And that's exactly what he did.

On his fifth play, Longley threw a 35-yard touchdown pass to Billy Joe DuPree. The score was now 16–10. On the Cowboys' next possession, Clint marched Dallas 70 yards down the field to the Washington 1-yard line. A handoff to Walt Garrison put Dallas in the lead 17–16.

With 13:27 left in the fourth quarter, former Cowboy Duane Thomas scored on a 19-yard run, putting Washington ahead 23–17.

On fourth and six, Longley threw to Bob Hayes for a first down at midfield. Two plays later and with 28 seconds left in the game, Clint threw a 50-yard pass over Washington's famed nickel defense, hitting Drew Pearson for a touchdown and the win. The Cowboys' bench went crazy.

Coach Landry was elated. It even made him happier when he saw the expression on George Allen's face. It was one of disbelief and disgust. It was a Thanksgiving Day to be thankful for.

Unfortunately for Clint Longley, his 15 minutes of fame ended with that game. Two seasons later he got into an argument with Roger Staubach and ended up punching him. He was then traded to the San Diego Chargers.

After Dallas failed to make the playoffs for the first time in nine years and ended the year with a mediocre 8–6 season, the press, among others, began to speculate that the Cowboys were beginning to look like an over-the-hill team, a team that could no longer win games. Coach Landry responded to the press at the Cowboys' end-of-season press conference by giving them his philosophy on the importance of winning:

I don't believe in winning at all costs, if that means cheating or doing things that are wrong. But if you think winning is not too important, then you are not willing to pay the price to win. Take away winning and you've taken away everything that is strong about America. If you don't believe in winning, you don't believe in free enterprise, capitalism, our way of life.

Our way of life means succeeding and you must win to do that. Today in America everything is "let's be free, let's be ourselves," but that eliminates responsibility. If you have freedom, you must have responsibility. If you are going to have free enterprise—have a country like ours—you've got to win, got to pay the price, got to do the things that make our country progressive. Once you start moving away from that—and that's what we're doing in America today—sooner or later you're going to fail. You won't remain strong.

This country is organized no differently from a football team. It's built on discipline, competition, and paying the price. Take away those things and you have chaos, weakness, and immorality—all the things that are taking place in America right now. So winning is important to America. It's got to be.

17

Farewells

MIDWAY THROUGH THE '74 SEASON I woke up in the middle of the night with excruciating pain in my neck. Even though I received treatment for the pain over the next few weeks, nothing could relieve it. Shortly thereafter it became so intense that I couldn't even attend practices.

Since traditional methods had proved unsuccessful, Dr. Knight decided it was time to take the next step: X-rays. Upon reviewing the films, he put my mind at ease by telling me there was no cause for alarm. He saw nothing in the X-rays that indicated there was a possibility for paralysis to set in—which was my biggest fear. He felt that the best way to deal with the pain was to inject Novocain directly into my trapezoid muscles in order to alleviate the spasms.

Instead, I developed a bleeding ulcer from the aspirin and dropped from 267 pounds to 247 pounds.

I survived the remainder of the season, but I had taken a great deal of aspirin to help with the pain. I was hesitant to take the drug codeine because it had caused a few of my teammates to develop kidney problems. Instead, I developed a bleeding ulcer from the aspirin and dropped from 267 pounds to 247 pounds.

After 14 seasons as a Dallas Cowboy, I decided that the 1974 season would be my last. Coach Landry attempted to get me to rescind my decision, but the aches and pains that had accompanied the gridiron battle had taken their toll, and I politely declined his offer. My retirement became official in July 1975.

To my surprise, though, I did suit up one last time. But instead of gutting it out on the field of Texas Stadium, I would be honored by the fans, my teammates, and the Murchison administration for my accomplishments as a Dallas Cowboy.

November 23, 1975, was officially named Bob Lilly Day at Texas Stadium, and that day I became the first member of the prestigious Ring of Honor.

They Took Away His Team

Following my retirement, Tom Landry went on to win Super Bowl XII by beating Denver 27–10 in January 1978. But on Thursday, February 23, 1989, Coach Landry's world would change forever.

The culmination of all their hopes, dreams, and memories had come to an end with a handshake, a few tears, and an emotional hug.

While he and his wife Alicia were watching the ten o'clock news, Coach learned that oilman Jerry Jones, president of Arkoma Exploration of Little Rock, Arkansas, had reached an agreement with Bum Bright to buy the Dallas Cowboys. It was also reported that Jones planned to bring in his good friend Jimmy Johnson, currently the head football coach at the University of Miami, to coach the Cowboys.

Bum Bright did not have the common courtesy to inform Coach or Tex Schramm as to what was going on before reporting it to the press. When Tex met with Coach, it was an emotional time for both of them.

They had been partners for 29 years, and they had built the Cowboys organization from scratch. They had shared losing as well as winning seasons, stood side by side on draft days, and celebrated Super Bowl victories together. The culmination of all their hopes, dreams, and memories had come to an end with a handshake, a few tears, and an emotional hug.

In the Dallas locker room, Landry met with his players for the very last time. He told them how much he would miss them. And then he began to cry. The players, through their own tears, responded by giving Coach a standing ovation.

When the press questioned Tom about his release he simply uttered, "They took away my team."

Upon hearing the news, Cowboys fans everywhere were infuriated with the lack of respect shown to Coach Landry, and they weren't afraid to show it. Within the NFL itself reaction to Tom's dismissal was swift and supportive. Commissioner Pete Rozelle said, "This is like [Vince] Lombardi's death."

Coach Landry wasn't afraid to show his frustration with the new organization either. The same year his tenure was terminated Landry turned down Jerry Jones's formal request to be inducted into the Ring of Honor. He continued to deny the Cowboys organization anything that required his presence or input for the next 18 years.

In 1990 Coach Tom Landry finally received his day in the sun when he was enshrined in the Pro Football Hall of Fame. His presenter was Roger Staubach. Roger epitomized what Landry thought a quarterback should be, so it was appropriate that he was the presenter on enshrinement day. Landry had been Roger's presenter when he was enshrined into the Hall of Fame in 1985 along with Frank Gatski, Joe Namath, Pete Rozelle, and the infamous O.J. Simpson.

Coach Landry's enshrinement class of 1990 was well represented by prestigious greats as well: Buck Buchanan, Bob Griese, Franco Harris, Ted Hendricks, Jack Lambert, and Bob St. Clair. It was a momentous occasion that Landry shared with his family, friends, former players, and coaches.

On November 7, 1993, at the request of Roger Staubach, Bob Hayes, Lee Roy Jordan, and myself, Coach was inducted into the Ring of Honor. He told us later that he felt "it was time to do it."

After 29 seasons as the Cowboys' head coach, Tom Landry finished his career with a 270–178–6 record.

The Death of a Legend

Coach was like a father to me after I retired, but while I was playing for him, he was that stone-faced man on the sideline who never allowed himself to get close to his players. I asked him why he was like that, and he replied, "You know, Bob, I'm the one that has to cut the players when it's time for them to go. You don't realize how hard that is for me to do. That's the one thing about this job I don't like. If I were to get close to someone on the team and then have to let him go, it would become a very difficult task for me to fulfill. I tried to keep my emotions and my distance from the players so if and when that day came that I needed to let them go, it wouldn't be as hard for me to do so. But when I think about that now, it's probably the one thing that I would have changed a bit."

Coach was like a father to me after I retired.

Although Coach kept a professional distance from his active players, he always made a point to call and encourage us after our playing careers ended. He wanted us to be as successful in life as we were on the playing field.

In May 1999 Coach was diagnosed with acute myelogenous leukemia, a rare form of the disease. He immediately began chemotherapy treatments. But less than one year later, on Saturday, February 12, 2000, at the age of 75, Thomas Wade Landry succumbed to the disease and quietly passed away at the Baylor University Medical Center.

The way he lived with faith and perseverance is an example of the great impact one man can make.

News of Tom's death caused an outpouring of deep sorrow and grief from his players and fans. He was loved and respected by so many people. At his funeral several of his former players gave tributes to the man in the fedora. There wasn't a dry eye in the room. He will be greatly missed by all.

For me, the man from Mission, Texas, has forever influenced my life. The way he lived with faith and perseverance is an example of the great impact one man can make. He was quite a guy, and he will forever remain in the hearts of those who had the privilege and blessing of playing for him.

18

Games I Will Never Forget

The Ice Bowl

There are some things in life that you never forget. For me personally, I will always remember November 22, 1963, the day President Kennedy was assassinated, and New Year's Eve 1967, the day we played the National Football League Championship Game against the Green Bay Packers on the "frozen tundra" of Lambeau Field. Due to the extreme weather conditions, the game became known as the Ice Bowl.

This was the second year in a row that the Cowboys and the Packers had played for the NFL championship. In 1966 Green Bay defeated us by a score of 34–27 on our final drive. We had four chances to score from the 2-yard line but just couldn't seem to get the job done. It was one of the most depressing losses I ever experienced. This game was not just between the Cowboys and the Packers; it was also a matchup of the two greatest minds in professional football—Tom Landry and Vince Lombardi.

That game remains the coldest NFL game on record. The official temperature at the start of the game was 13 degrees below zero with a windchill factor of minus-48 degrees. It was so cold that the field's new $80,000 heating system shut down. The playing surface was as hard as cement and slick with ice. But none of that seemed to bother the 50,861 screaming Packers fans as they sat in the frozen stands rooting for their team.

Even the officials were affected by the cold. When the referee blew his metal whistle to signal the start of play on the opening kickoff, it froze to his lips. When he tried to remove it, he tore the skin from his mouth. For the remainder of the game, the officials had to verbally end plays. I can only imagine the condition of their throats and voices at the end of the game.

When the referee blew his metal whistle to signal the start of play on the opening kickoff, it froze to his lips.

That day several players suffered frostbite from the freezing conditions. Jethro Pugh still suffers mild effects from the exposure he received that day, and Don Meredith developed pneumonia and had to be hospitalized upon his return to Texas.

The halftime entertainment (the Wisconsin State University–La Crosse Marching Chiefs Band) was canceled because the woodwind instruments froze up, and the mouthpieces of the brass instruments stuck to the players' lips. Seven band members developed hypothermia and were hospitalized. And that was all before the game even started!

In the locker room before the game, I put on all the clothes I could find. I first put on my Long Handles, then plastic-wrapped my feet and put on a second pair of socks. Our assistant coach, Ernie Stautner, wouldn't let us wear gloves on the field. He said, "Men don't wear gloves in this league."

We went back out on the field and every guy on the Packers' team had gloves on. We ended up with frostbite, not to mention we practically froze to death.

At the beginning of the first quarter, the field was not yet completely frozen and our cleats still caught the turf when we ran. But by the end of the quarter, I had to remove my cleats and replace them with soccer shoes. We were sliding all over the place. By the end of the game, Lambeau Field was a solid sheet of ice.

The game began and Green Bay drew first blood after moving the ball 82 yards in 16 plays and capping it off with an eight-yard touchdown pass from Bart Starr to wide receiver Boyd Dowler. During that drive, Dallas was called for pass interference and defensive holding.

In the second quarter Starr once again hit Dowler for a 46-yard touchdown, making the score 14–0. But two costly Green Bay turnovers resulted in Dallas putting 10 unanswered points on the board.

Our defensive tackle, Willie Townes, forced the first fumble when he sacked Starr for a loss and the ball came loose. Our defensive end, George Andrie, recovered the ball and ran it in seven yards for a touchdown. The second fumble occurred when Packers safety Willie Wood fumbled the ball after signaling for a fair catch. Our rookie defensive back, Phil Clark, recovered the ball at the 17-yard line of Green Bay. We were unsuccessful in our attempt to get into the end zone, but our kicker, Danny Villanueva, kicked a 21-yard field goal, making the score 14–10 at the half.

At the beginning of the third quarter the temperature dropped to 20 below zero, and the windchill factor dropped to more than 40 below. The ground was frozen solid. Neither the Packers nor the Cowboys were able to score any points in the third quarter.

In the first play of the fourth quarter, running back Dan Reeves threw a 50-yard pass to wide receiver Lance Rentzel on a half-back option play for a touchdown, and we took the lead at 17–14.

Later in the quarter Green Bay kicker Don Chandler missed a 40-yard field-goal attempt.

With 4:50 left on the clock, Bart Starr took over on his own 32-yard line. He led his team down the field with three strategic completions. The first was a 13-yard pass to Dowler, the second was a 12-yard pass to running back Donny Anderson, and the third was a 19-yard throw to fullback Chuck Mercein.

On the next play Mercein was again given the ball, and he ran eight yards to a first down on the Cowboys' 3-yard line. Donny Anderson twice attempted to run the ball into the end zone, but our defense stopped him both times on the 1-yard line.

On third and goal with 16 seconds left in the game, Starr called for the Packers' final timeout. He met with Coach Lombardi on the sideline to discuss which play would be called. The tension was so thick you could cut it with a knife. Bart returned to the field, and after taking the snap he ran a one-yard quarterback sneak behind center Ken Bowman. Green Bay guard Jerry Kramer blocked our defensive tackle Jethro Pugh, allowing Starr to score the winning touchdown. Final score: Packers 21, Cowboys 17.

This game was truly a game of inches. At the sound of the final gun, the Cowboys came within six inches of winning.

According to David Maraniss, author of the 1999 book *When Pride Still Mattered: A Life of Vince Lombardi*, Coach Lombardi was anxious to get the game over with before the conditions became worse. Rather than attempting a field goal, which could only tie the game and prolong the grueling conditions, Starr was told to call a handoff to Mercein. That's exactly what he did, but unbeknownst to the other 10 guys in the huddle, Starr decided that he would keep the ball himself and avoid the risk of a fumble. The rest is history.

After the game, the Cowboys' locker room was quiet and somber. Many of the players held their heads in their hands. I don't recall Coach Landry saying anything to anybody.

I went in to take a shower and the water temperature felt hot, but in reality it was only about 60 degrees. When we finally took off for Dallas in that warm 727 airplane, I thanked the Lord that we were out of there. All I remember about the ride home was the deafening silence and the fact that I got out of there alive.

All I remember about the ride home was the deafening silence and the fact that I got out of there alive.

Because of the horrific conditions that day, George Andrie, Dick Daniels, Jethro Pugh, Mel Renfro, and Willie Townes were all treated for frostbite, and quarterback Don Meredith did not recover from his bout with pneumonia until the following February.

Before I played this game, I smoked many cigars and cigarettes—and inhaled both. After that game, my lungs were in very bad shape and have not been the same since. I quit smoking altogether and cannot stand to even be in a room where smoking is taking place. Even inhaling the exhaust from cars and trucks causes me to have breathing problems.

The one positive that came out of this game is that a total of 13 members from both teams would later become enshrined into the Pro Football Hall of Fame.

From the Cowboys: general manager Tex Schramm, coach Tom Landry, defensive back Mel Renfro, offensive lineman Rayfield Wright, and myself.

From the Packers: coach Vince Lombardi, quarterback Bart Starr, offensive lineman Forrest Gregg, defensive back Herb Adderley, defensive back Willie Wood, defensive lineman Willie Davis, linebacker Ray Nitschke, and defensive lineman Henry Jordan.

The *Monday Night Football* Massacre

In 1970 we played the St. Louis Cardinals on *Monday Night Football* in front of 69,323 fans at the Cotton Bowl. It was the first Monday night game that the Cowboys had ever played. We were totally humiliated, as the Cardinals beat us 38–0 in front of the entire nation.

Before the game I heard Larry Wilson, the Cardinals free safety, say that St. Louis was out to prove that the 20–7 victory over us earlier in the season was no fluke. He was certainly right about that.

During the game Meredith was up in the press booth doing the color commentary for ABC with his *Monday Night Football* partners, Keith Jackson and Howard Cosell, when all of a sudden the fans started chanting, "We want Meredith! We want Meredith!" These were probably the same fans who used to boo Don in his early years as a Cowboy.

I later found out that Don was quoted as saying, "The Cowboys' players are without a leader." There was no doubt that we lacked leadership in this game!

In the first period our punter, Ron Widby, kicked a line drive that was returned 74 yards for a touchdown by Johnny Roland—who later scored again from the 10- and 3-yard lines.

With the score 17–0 and seven minutes left in the third quarter, Cornell Green intercepted the ball from Cardinals tight end Jackie Smith and ran it to the St. Louis 5-yard line. The guy who caught Cornell was Jim Hart, the quarterback! A defensive back never wants to get caught by a quarterback.

With a first down at the 5, we failed to score. First Calvin Hill was hit for an eight-yard loss. Next, Walt Garrison ran, claiming only one yard. And finally, Craig Morton, who was unable to pass, maneuvered his way to the Cardinals 3. On fourth down

Craig's pass to Pettis Norman was knocked down by corner-back Roger Wehrli, who ended up intercepting three of Morton's passes throughout the day. That basically summed up the entire rushing and passing game for the Cowboys—pathetic!

Super Bowl V

Unlike the Ice Bowl title game of 1967, Super Bowl V (also known as the Blooper Bowl) was played on January 17, 1971, in the balmy 70-degree temperature of the Orange Bowl in Miami, Florida.

This was the first Super Bowl to be played after the merger of the American Football League and the National Football League. All 26 AFL and NFL teams were divided into two conferences with 13 teams in each conference. The Browns, Steelers, and Colts of the NFL joined the 10 other teams from the AFL, which became the American Football Conference (AFC). The other 13 NFL teams formed the National Football Conference (NFC). Incidentally, this is why the Colts represented the NFL in Super Bowl III and the AFC in Super Bowl V.

The press called this game "a match between an upstart team and a seasoned franchise." The upstart team they were referring to was the Cowboys, while the seasoned franchise was the Baltimore Colts, led by quarterback great Johnny Unitas.

Turnovers, controversial plays, and referee calls that never seemed to go our way were a few of the many mishaps that the Cowboys experienced that day. By the end of the game, we held the Super Bowl record of 11 combined turnovers for both teams.

That wasn't all that deflated the Cowboys' spirit. Before the team even set foot on Florida soil we lost our fullback and second-leading Cowboys rusher, Calvin Hill, who was out for the year after suffering a severe leg injury late in the regular season. Then there was the wire-service story that alleged that many members of the Cowboys' team had been involved in drug use. Our wide receiver, Lance Rentzel, was found guilty on a morals charge. And last, but definitely not least, the quarterback controversy between Morton and Staubach had yet to be resolved. Even though the media depicted the Cowboys as a troubled team, they still had us favored over the Colts by two.

In the locker room the team was getting psychologically prepared for the game. Some of the players were sitting in front of their lockers contemplating strategies to beat their opponent. I paced back and forth contemplating my own strategies and wondering whether or not today would be the day that we would finally win the big one.

A thunderous roar of 79,204 people shook the Orange Bowl as the referee announced that Dallas won the coin toss. We chose to receive.

In the beginning I guess both teams were a little anxious because the first three possessions of the game ended with punts. Each team went three and out. Finally, on the first play of the Colts' second drive, our linebacker Chuck Howley intercepted a Johnny Unitas pass and returned it 22 yards to the Baltimore 46. But we were unable to score because of a holding penalty and ended up punting. Colts' punt returner Ron Gardin fumbled the punt, and our safety, Cliff Harris, recovered the ball at the Baltimore 9-yard line. Dallas was unable to put six points up on the board and had to settle for a 14-yard field goal by our kicker, Mike Clark, giving us a 3–0 lead in the first quarter.

Later in the quarter Craig Morton hit Bob Hayes for a 41-yard pass to the Colts' 12-yard line. The referees tacked on a roughing the passer penalty, putting the ball on the six. Even with the help of the penalty, we were still unable to score a touchdown. On first down Morton's pass was deflected by Ted Hendricks; on second down, the first play of the second quarter, Duane Thomas was tackled for a one-yard loss; and on third down Craig was charged with an intentional grounding penalty, forcing the Cowboys back to the 22-yard line. Again, we had to settle for a 30-yard field goal by Mike Clark, making the score Dallas 6, Baltimore 0.

We kicked off, and Baltimore's defensive back, Jim Duncan, returned the ball 22 yards to the Colts' 25-yard line. After throwing two incompletions, Unitas dropped back and found wide receiver Eddie Hinton, but the pass was both high and behind him. Hinton leaped up and tipped the ball, changing its trajectory. The ball was then allegedly tipped by our defensive back Mel Renfro (conclusive evidence was never shown either way that he had ever touched the ball) and fell into the arms of Baltimore tight end John Mackey, who took the ball 75 yards for a touchdown. With Jim O'Brien missing the extra point, which was blocked by Mark Washington, the score was tied 6–6.

With nine minutes to go in the second quarter, Johnny Unitas fumbled the ball after being tackled by linebacker Lee Roy Jordan. This set up a seven-yard touchdown pass from Morton to Thomas, giving Dallas the lead, 13–6.

When the Colts again regained possession, Unitas threw a pass that was intercepted by Mel Renfro. During that play John was hit by George Andrie and was knocked out of the game with a rib injury and replaced by Earl Morrall. Again, the Cowboys came away without any points scored.

After the punt, Morrall threw two passes for 47 yards. Lee Roy Jordan was called for a personal foul, which put the Colts on the

Cowboys' 2-yard line. With less than two minutes to go in the half, the Colts failed to score.

Even though neither team scored in the third quarter, NFL Films was able to obtain enough footage to complete another episode of *The NFL's Greatest Follies.*

On the opening kickoff of the second half, Baltimore's Jim Duncan fumbled the ball, Dallas recovered, and the Cowboys moved the ball to the Colts' 1-yard line. Taking the handoff on the one, Duane Thomas fumbled, and the ball was recovered by Jim Duncan. The Colts' next drive was to the Cowboys' 44-yard line, but Jim O'Brien missed the 52-yard field-goal attempt. The ball fell short of the goal post, and defensive back Mel Renfro let the ball bounce, assuming it would go into the end zone for a touchdown. It ended up settling on the 1-yard line, and Baltimore center Tom Goode downed it.

The Cowboys went three and out, and on the punt Colts rookie running back Jack Maitland was called for a 15-yard clipping penalty. Baltimore made it to the Cowboys' 11-yard line, but on the first play of the fourth quarter, an Earl Morrall pass was intercepted by Chuck Howley in the end zone. Again, the Cowboys ended up punting.

On first down and on their own 18-yard line, Morrall threw an incomplete pass. On the next play he fumbled the snap but was able to recover it and threw the ball away, thereby avoiding a loss of yards. On third down, Morrall once again threw an incompletion, but due to the pass interference penalty called on Mel Renfro (who was covering Eddie Hinton), the Colts were awarded a first down.

The next Colts drive went down in Super Bowl history. The Colts were on the Dallas 30-yard line when they decided to go with a flea-flicker play. Morrall handed off to running back

Sam Havrilak, who was supposed to throw it back to Morrall. But before he could release the ball, Jethro Pugh came charging toward him, forcing Havrilak to throw the ball to John Mackey. In the meantime, Eddie Hinton cut in front of Mackey and made the catch. As he took off toward the end zone, Hinton fumbled the ball at the 10-yard line when he was tackled by defensive back Cornell Green. Both teams scrambled to recover the ball, but it rolled through the end zone for a touchback, giving Dallas the ball at their own 20-yard line.

> *I ripped off my helmet and hurled it 40 yards downfield in frustration.*

The Cowboys' possession was short-lived. Three plays later, Craig Morton threw an interception to Colts safety Rick Volk, who returned the ball to the Cowboys' 3-yard line. Two plays later Nowatzke rushed for two yards and scored six more points for Baltimore. The extra point was good and the game was once again tied at 13–13.

After only three plays and with two minutes left in the game, Dallas forced the Colts to punt. The kick was short and the Cowboys gained possession on the Colts' 48-yard line. On second down, Craig Morton threw a pass that was intended for Dan Reeves but landed in the arms of Baltimore linebacker Mike Curtis, who returned the ball to the Cowboys' 28-yard line. Two plays later, Jim O'Brien kicked the game-winning field goal, giving the Colts the lead at 16–13.

When I saw the ball travel through the goal posts, I became enraged. I ripped off my helmet and hurled it 40 yards downfield in frustration. When it hit the artificial turf, the pads and chin strap broke free. I had waited 11 years for this victory, and to have it taken away in the final seconds of the game was more than I could bear.

A young rookie from Baltimore brought my helmet back to me and said, "Mr. Lilly, here's your helmet." I took the helmet from him and politely said, "Thank you." I really felt ashamed of what I had done. It would have been horrible if I had hurt someone. It was a spontaneous act and not one that I am proud of.

With a short kick from O'Brien and less than five seconds left in the game, the Cowboys got the ball back on our own 40. Morton quickly stepped back to pass to Walt Garrison but was intercepted by Colts safety Jerry Logan at the Baltimore 29-yard line. Time ran out on us.

The one positive to come from all of this is that Chuck Howley received the MVP award for intercepting two passes and recovering a fumble. It was the first time the award had been presented to a defensive player and the first and only time to a member of the losing team.

Super Bowl VI

We finished the 1971 regular season 11–3. In the first playoff round we destroyed the Vikings by a score of 20–12 and then went on to beat the 49ers 14–3 for the NFC title and the right to return to the Super Bowl. But after both postseason victories, there was no celebration in the locker room. We had celebrated before, only to be shut down later. Our goal this time was to win the Super Bowl.

Our first trip to the Super Bowl was quite different from the second. In Super Bowl V we were in awe of the hundreds of reporters shoving microphones and cameras in our faces, the daily two-hour press conferences, and the people who were constantly asking us for autographs. It was a zoo! We really weren't ready for all the hoopla, but this time we knew what to expect and were able to concentrate on the game.

It was a clear, 39-degree day on January 16, 1972, in the city of New Orleans. Tulane Stadium, the old Sugar Bowl, was the site for Super Bowl VI, and the Cowboys came ready to play. We were more confident and more relaxed than we had been for the previous Super Bowl. Maybe it's because we had already been there and knew what to expect. But there was something different about the players that day. You could see it in their eyes— nothing short of winning would be acceptable.

In front of 81,023 screaming fans, the Dolphins won the coin toss and elected to receive. As in Super Bowl V, anxiety had set in, and neither team could move the ball on first possession.

On the first play of the Dolphins' second possession, Larry Csonka ran a sweep and gained 12 yards. Unbeknownst to him, it would be his longest of the day. On the next play, Csonka fumbled (his first fumble all year) and the ball was recovered by our linebacker Chuck Howley at the Cowboys' 48-yard line. We moved the ball down the field but had to settle for a nine-yard field goal by Mike Clark. The quarter ended with Dallas 3, Miami 0, reminiscent of Super Bowl V.

On the third play of Miami's next possession at their own 38-yard line, I chased and sacked quarterback Bob Griese for a 29-yard loss. It was the longest quarterback sack in Super Bowl history and also my second Super Bowl record—the first being my helmet toss in Super Bowl V.

It was the longest quarterback sack in Super Bowl history.

Early in the second quarter, Miami drove to the Cowboys' 42-yard line. But they ended up with no points after Miami kicker Garo Yepremian missed a 49-yard field-goal attempt.

Later in the second quarter, the Cowboys drove 69 yards in nine plays. Then, on a seven-yard touchdown pass from Roger Staubach to Lance Alworth, we increased our lead over Miami by a score of 10–0.

With only 1:11 left in the half, Bob Griese passed twice to receiver Paul Warfield and once to running back Jim Kiick for a total of 39 yards. On the Dallas 24-yard line, Griese threw again to Warfield, who was open at the 2-yard line, only to have it deflected by Cornell Green. Miami had to settle for three.

Going into the second half with a 10–3 lead, the Cowboys came on to the field really smokin'. We totally dominated the remainder of the game and completely shut down the Miami offense.

Dallas opened up the third quarter with a 71-yard, eight-play drive that ended in a three-yard sweep and touchdown by Duane Thomas, making the score 17–3. Totally fired up, the defensive unit never allowed Miami a single first down the entire third quarter.

In the fourth quarter, Chuck Howley ended a Miami drive by intercepting a pass from Bob Griese to Jim Kiick and returning it 41 yards to the Miami 9-yard line. Three plays later, Staubach hit tight end Mike Ditka for a seven-yard touchdown, making it Dallas 24, Miami 3. With 12 minutes left in the game, we were beginning to realize that our day had finally come.

In the final minutes of the game, Miami gave it one last try. In a drive that began on their own 23-yard line, Griese fumbled the snap, and the ball was recovered by Cowboys end Larry Cole at the Dallas 20-yard line. However, on first and goal at the 1-yard line, Calvin Hill fumbled while attempting to dive across the goal line. The ball was recovered by Dolphins defensive tackle Manny Fernandez, but time had run out for Miami, and the game was over.

To say I was elated would be an understatement. We had finally won the big one and would no longer be called next year's champs or the bridesmaids of the NFL. In an interview with the press, Cornell Green summoned it up perfectly, saying, "The difference between the Dolphins and Cowboys was that the

Dolphins were just happy to be in the game and the Cowboys came to win the game."

Roger was named the Super Bowl's Most Valuable Player. He completed 12 out of 19 passes for 119 yards, threw two touchdown passes, and rushed five times for 18 yards.

The scene in the locker room was not one you would expect after winning a Super Bowl. Guys weren't running around yelling and pouring champagne over everyone, Landry wasn't thrown into the showers, and no one tried to "pants" the TV crew. I think the emotions that were displayed were those of relief. We'd finally done it—the Cowboys were the world champions.

Third Quarter

Characters, Heroes, and Great Leading Men

19

The Originals

THE IDEA OF BUILDING A TEAM FROM SCRATCH intrigued Coach Landry. He always said that the key to success for any professional football team was the presence of young players. But there was just one problem. They were unable to participate in the 1960 college draft because it was held *before* the team was officially admitted to the league.

Due to the foresight of expansion committee head George Halas, the Rangers (as they were called then) were able to sign two talented college seniors. The first was SMU's quarterback Don Meredith and the second was University of New Mexico running back Don Perkins. The rest of the Dallas team would eventually come from a hastily compiled list of disgruntled players submitted by the coaches of the existing NFL teams. Many of the players were 30 or older. Fullback Ed Modzelewski of Cleveland and center Charlie Ane from Detroit both chose retirement rather than report to an expansion team that was starting from scratch. Many were unhappy with their status on their former teams and were content to get a fresh start with Dallas, especially those who were Texans—they were finally coming home.

Tex Schramm knew that if he drafted players who had graduated from colleges in Texas, he would have a commonality with them and a better chance of keeping them happy to be a part of an expansion team. His first choice was running back Don McIlhenny from the Packers' draft list. He was elated to be coming home to Texas.

Middle linebacker Jack Patera was just happy to get out of the Chicago Cardinals organization and be given an opportunity to start over again.

Tight end Dick Bielski from the Eagles and guard Bob Fry from the Rams were also headed for Dallas. Both felt that the hardest thing about going to an expansion team was that everything was different—the players, the coaches, and the ideas on how to put together a team from scratch.

Linebacker Jerry Tubbs had been considering retirement when coach Red Hickey of the San Francisco 49ers put his name on the expansion list in 1959. Jerry told Schramm that he was planning to leave football and go to work for the Coca-Cola company. When the Coke deal fell through, Tubbs decided to sign with the Cowboys.

The players who signed with the Cowboys in their inaugural year had more in common than not. Because many of them were

The players who signed with the Cowboys in their inaugural year had more in common than not.

children of the Depression era, they were hardworking, honest, and self-sufficient. They knew what the words "hard times" really meant.

Jerry Tubbs was raised in the Texas dust bowl of the 1930s, playing on a relatively successful football team in Breckenridge, Texas. Former Detroit Lions defensive end Gene Cronin's family escaped the dust bowl of Nebraska only to find that California wasn't much better; his father became a ditch digger, and the family lived in a tent. Defensive end John Gonzaga never went to college and instead was forced to work in the steel mills. Gonzaga,

132

like Tubbs, was another 49er who was extremely bitter toward his former coach, Red Hickey, for putting his name on the expansion team list. Fullback Gene Babb lost both parents by the time he was 13 and, again, it was Red Hickey who sent him to Dallas.

But the one who would cause Tom Landry the most problems was end Ray Mathews from the Pittsburgh Steelers. He was the most bitter for being cut and the most disrespectful to Coach Landry. After playing nine years with the Steelers, he came to Dallas with a chip on his shoulder. He did everything he could to get the team to send him back to Pittsburgh, but they never did.

The quarterback position had been filled by former Giants player Don Heinrich. Don saw limited action with the Giants, playing behind starter Charley Conerly for most of his career. Both Tex and Coach didn't feel that Heinrich was talented enough to start every game and the rookie Meredith didn't have the experience. Enter Eddie LeBaron.

Schramm was able to talk Eddie out of retiring while making a deal with George Marshall and his Redskins. The Cowboys would trade their first- and sixth-round draft choices in the 1961 draft to Washington for the rights to the diminutive, four-time Pro Bowl player Eddie LeBaron. LeBaron would go on to be the starting quarterback for the Dallas team for the next three years.

Jerry Tubbs

In the beginning the Cowboys roster was made up of players who were in the twilight of their careers. I was sure happy to find a few exceptions, like Jerry Tubbs.

Jerry may have had a few problems with his back and his knee, but he was exactly what Coach Landry was looking for in a middle linebacker—he was smart and a tremendous competitor.

He was so good that he would often make 30 or 40 tackles in a game.

He was so good that he would often make 30 or 40 tackles in a game. A team leader, Tom appointed him first as a player/coach, and after his retirement he made Jerry his assistant coach, where he remained for the next 22 years.

In 1954 Jerry went to the University of Oklahoma to play football as a middle linebacker for coach Bud Wilkinson. After playing on two back-to-back, undefeated national championship teams, he was drafted number one by the Chicago Cardinals in 1957.

His rookie year, Jerry signed with the Cardinals for a $9,000 salary and a $2,000 bonus. The coaches felt that at 215 pounds, he was too small to play middle linebacker. They moved him to outside linebacker, where he became a starter. Three-quarters of the way through the season the Cards sent him to San Francisco, where he played outside linebacker for coach Frankie Albert.

When coach Red Hickey arrived on the scene, Jerry was again playing middle linebacker. He decided to retire in 1959 to take a job with Coca-Cola. When that fell through, he came to Dallas.

Jerry joined the team in 1960 and was one of those guys who had no problem sleeping on an airplane or hitting somebody on the football field. Those first couple of years I felt sorry for Jerry. For a rookie, learning Coach Landry's system was extremely difficult. There were a few of us, including me, who weren't doing their jobs and Jerry would have to cover for all of us while trying to play his own position. When I would forget to close off my man, Jerry would yell, "Lilly, close the trap. You're going to get me killed!"

He was a natural leader in 1967 and made a smooth transition to assistant coach, working with the linebackers. Jerry was ideal for the job—knowledgeable, patient, and a good teacher. And having played middle linebacker, he knew the Cowboys defense and the responsibility of each position.

Eddie LeBaron

When I met Eddie LeBaron I thought, "How can he play quarterback? He's so short, and the guys rushing him are so big." Then I watched him handle the ball, and I knew how he had lasted so long in the NFL.

For the Cowboys' first three seasons, Eddie was the starting quarterback. He was the perfect guy for the position. First of all, he was intelligent. He had graduated from George Washington University's School of Law and had recently passed both the Texas and California bar exams. He also had service experience, which made him a respected team leader and gridiron general. He may not have been in his prime, but he still had plenty left in him to do the job.

Sometimes when the opposing linemen were bearing down on him, he would completely disappear from sight, then all of a sudden you would see the football soar out from this wall of jerseys and he would hit his man.

His favorite wide receiver was Frank Clarke. I guess you could say that they were the Montana/Rice combination of their day.

Eddie came from the wine country of northern California—Sonoma County. He attended the University of the Pacific (UOP) as a freshman at age 16. He was extremely intelligent for his age.

Eddie's first coach at Pacific was Amos Alonzo Stagg, who at that time was 84 years old. Still incorporating the old spread, single-wing formations, UOP was getting pounded by teams who utilized the T formation. Coach Stagg retired the following year and was replaced by his assistant, Larry Siemering.

UOP had winning seasons throughout the years that Eddie played with them. He later went on to play with John Brodie in the East-West Game, where he was named MVP, and after that in the very first Senior Bowl. In the All-Star Game against the Philadelphia Eagles, the college All-Stars won. On that same All-Star team was R.C. Owens, Doak Walker, Charlie Justice, and Art Weiner.

LeBaron was the number one draft choice in 1950 in a secret draft by the 49ers of the AAFC. He chose not to go. He was later drafted by the Redskins in the 10th round, but because he had been a marine reservist, he was called upon by the Corps to fight in Korea. And fight he did. Wounded twice during the war, Eddie was decorated with two Purple Hearts, a Bronze Star, and a Letter of Commendation for his heroic actions on the front lines.

When Eddie showed up at training camp, Coach Landry introduced him to his offensive system. Eddie thought that it would be too hard for the guys to learn, but Coach told him that he needed to compete with the Giants and Cleveland. He explained to LeBaron that once the team got the talent they needed, they would be able to beat those teams, but first the system would have to be in place. Eddie agreed.

Eddie was the Cowboys' starting quarterback throughout the team's first three years in the NFL (1960 to 1962) and started once in 1963. He was selected for the Pro Bowl four times (1955, 1957, 1958, and 1962) and was the leading NFL passer in 1958.

Eddie LeBaron was respected by his teammates for his skill and great athletic ability. He proved that size was not a factor in the world of professional football.

Frank Clarke

Frank Clarke was truly a gentlemen's gentleman. Like Jerry Tubbs, Frank was an exception among the 36 veterans the Cowboys picked from the NFL expansion pool.

Frank Clarke was truly a gentlemen's gentleman.

In the 1956 NFL draft, he was drafted in the fifth round by Cleveland. He came to us from the Browns and was happy to get a chance at a fresh start. At 6′0″ and 215 pounds, the 26-year-old receiver impressed Coach Landry and Tex Schramm with his size and speed.

A big play receiver with good speed, Frank played longer than any of the other originals—all the way through to 1967. He currently holds the franchise record of 14 touchdown receptions for the organization.

When he first came to Dallas he had been tagged by the Browns as an unfulfilled promise. But he soon proved that tag to be a myth. The Frank Clarke I knew took some tremendous hits and kept going. He was well respected by Coach Landry and his teammates, for he gave his very best a hundred percent of the time.

From 1961 though 1964, Frank, as a receiver, led the Cowboys in yards and touchdowns. In 1962 he became the team's first 1,000-yard receiver; in 1963 and 1964 he led them in receptions; and in 1964 Frank was named an All-Pro.

On September 23, 1962, Frank was part of an infamous play where, for the first time in an NFL game, points were awarded for a penalty. After he scored on a 99-yard touchdown pass from Eddie LeBaron, the Cowboys were caught holding in the end zone and Pittsburgh was awarded a safety. The Steelers won the game, 30–28.

Frank was known for his ability to catch long passes. One of his most famous catches was in our first championship game against Green Bay in the Cotton Bowl in 1966.

Even though I blocked the Packers' extra point, they were still ahead, 34–20. With only four minutes left to play in the game, Don Meredith threw a pass behind the secondary, hitting Frank for the touchdown. The score was now 34–27. In our next and final possession, we threatened to score but came up a couple of yards short. Even though we lost, Frank played a great game. He retired after the 1967 season.

Don Perkins

In 1960 Gil Brandt signed two of the top college seniors in the country. One was quarterback Don Meredith and the other was running back Don Perkins.

Perkins came out of New Mexico State, and Dallas signed him to a personal-service contract at the request of New Mexico senator Clinton Anderson, who was a personal friend of Clint Murchison.

While Meredith was widely known throughout the Dallas area, Don was relatively unknown. Despite his College All-Star status, Don was a relatively quiet and unselfish man, but when he stepped foot on the gridiron, he was explosive.

One time Don was helping a rookie running back who was basically after his job. When Walt Garrison asked Perkins why he would do such a thing, Don responded, "If you're a better player than I am, then you should be playing. If you're not better than I am, then I should be playing." It was as simple as that.

Along with Frank Clarke and Don Bishop, Perkins was one of the African American pioneers of the Cowboys organization. He arrived in Dallas during the final days of the Jim Crow laws.

When he first reported to training camp he was extremely overweight, but he returned in '61 ready to play the fullback position at a slender, strong 195 pounds.

Perk was a tremendous competitor. He wasn't extremely fast, but he had great acceleration. Even if there wasn't much of a hole, he could burst through the line and still make yards. He was also a great blocker and could block linebackers and ends who out-weighed him by 30 to 60 pounds. Don was proof that you didn't have to be big to be great. He was voted to six Pro Bowl teams.

Don was proof that you didn't have to be big to be great.

In 1976 I had the honor of inducting Don Perkins into the Ring of Honor alongside his quarterback, Don Meredith.

PERKINS'S STORIES

On the first day of the first Dallas Cowboys training camp at Forest Grove, Oregon, in 1960, Don Perkins was on his hands and knees, coughing and gagging as he crawled across the field after a disastrous showing in the Landry Mile. Coach had every-one run it to test each player's condition. At that time, Don's wasn't up to par.

After the run he had a meeting with Coach. It was there that he learned the value of Tom's patience and ability to recognize potential. In 1962, Don went on to become the first Cowboy to make All-NFL.

A few years later, we were playing a game against Atlanta, and Don was facing Tommy Nobis, the number one draft choice of the Falcons and an All-American linebacker from Texas. Don was picking up Nobis on the blitz most of the game, but Tommy beat him one time. Coach shouted from the sideline, "Perkins! That's your man!" It was uncharacteristic of Tom to yell like that.

Don pulled himself up and yelled back, "Hell, I know it!"

It wasn't that Don didn't know that Nobis was his man, it was just that this mammoth of a linebacker whipped him on that play. But Don shrugged it off and kept playing. He probably felt he had one coming for that time years ago when he screwed up the Landry Mile.

Bob Fry

Bob was an offensive lineman and a connoisseur of Western novels who came to us from the Los Angeles Rams. The Rams drafted him in 1953 out of Kentucky. He always looked too light for an offensive tackle, but he'd played well for seven years with L.A.

Ole Bob weighed only 235 pounds and wore a corset for a bad back, but he was a master at holding. He camouflaged his hands, allowing his opponent to get right up against him before he grabbed him. He'd even fall down with a guy, making it look like he was the one being run over.

Before we were to play the Steelers, Bob knew he would be going up against his nemesis, Ernie Stautner. He wanted to prepare himself for the game, so he would have the defense constantly hit him in the head during practice because Ernie was a master of the head slap. He figured that if we toughened him up enough, Ernie wouldn't be able to get to him.

Before weigh-ins, he would carry weights in his boxer shorts in order to give him an extra 10 pounds on the scales.

Mike Connelly

Mike was in his rookie season with the Rams when the Cowboys acquired him in 1960. He played center for Utah State and enlisted in the marines before joining the NFL.

Even though he was extremely self-disciplined and tough, Mike weighed only about 225 pounds. Before weigh-ins, he would carry weights in his boxer shorts in order to give him an extra 10 pounds on the scales. He played for Dallas for eight years—all the time taking vitamins, drinking milkshakes, and eating every chance he could in order to keep his weight up.

Jim Doran

Jim was the first Cowboy to be named to the Pro Bowl. For nine years he played end for the Detroit Lions before coming to the Cowboys in the 1960 expansion draft. In his first year with Dallas, he led the team with 31 catches and 554 yards. I spent only one year with Jim, as he retired after the 1961 season.

Bill Howton

Billy was a favorite receiver of both Eddie LeBaron and Don Meredith. After seven successful years with the Green Bay Packers and one year with Cleveland, Billy signed with the Cowboys in 1960. Howton was a former All-American from Rice and was selected twice as an All-Pro. He retired from the Cowboys in 1963.

Don Meredith

Owner Clint Murchison was determined to have Mount Vernon's favorite son as the quarterback for his new franchise. Don Meredith was an All-American out of SMU. In 1960, the league assigned Meredith's rights to Dallas. That was part of the deal that was agreed upon between the expansion team committee, the other NFL owners, and Clint Murchison. Don signed a personal-service contract believed to be worth more than $100,000 over three years.

Don used to say, "I had the best contract in football. Tex Schramm reminded me of that every time we talked about it."

If ever a nickname fit someone, it was Meredith's—"Dandy Don." He was also the player who frustrated Coach Landry the most. He decided that he would be the quarterback of his own life, and he certainly was. Someone had to be in charge of it. He was not the type of person to give control of his life to anyone—and that meant not to Jesus and not to Coach Landry. Don's belief system was simple…you only go around once in life, so enjoy every minute of every day, and have as much fun as you possibly can.

He decided that he would be the quarterback of his own life, and he certainly was.

Coach saw Don as a sinner and a rebel. Don used to tell Tom that he considered himself the reincarnation of Bobby Layne. Meredith had many of Layne's vices, like drinking, partying, and chasing women. He used to tell Tom, "When I die, I want to come back as Bobby Layne's chauffeur." That used to drive Coach crazy! The two fought for nine years.

Many of Don's teammates may not have agreed with his lifestyle, but they sure respected and admired him on the football field. He kept the team loose. We all loved to hear him sing country western songs.

One thing for sure, Don was one tough Texan. He was by far the toughest quarterback I ever played with. I never saw anyone take a beating like he did, get himself up, and return directly to the huddle. I've seen him get hit so hard that it knocked the wind out of him. When he returned to the huddle he would whisper to one of us to call the play because he physically couldn't speak. Leaving the game was unthinkable.

In those early days when we had such bad teams, he made us laugh, always fooling around. In practice he would come out of the huddle singing "I Didn't Know God Made Honky-Tonk Angels."

A few times he would call a play using various names of fruit.

He'd get under center and yell, "Apples! Oranges! Peaches!"—and finally—"Bananas!" They'd snap the ball, and we'd all crack up. Well, everyone but Coach Landry.

One time we were playing Pittsburgh, and Don was getting killed by the Steelers' defensive line. They were really a tough team back in the early 1960s. Pittsburgh, along with the Cleveland Browns, used to be in our division until they joined the AFC as part of the merger.

Throughout the game, Meredith was having a pretty tough time because the Steelers' defensive linemen were breaking through our offensive line and just pounding him, especially Ernie Stautner, who at that time was Pittsburgh's toughest defensive tackle (and future Cowboys defensive line coach). His only goal during the game was to pound the quarterback and head slap him in the process. In fact, I think this was the game where Ernie broke Meredith's nose.

Back in those days the hash marks were about fifteen yards from our benches. When the players lined up on the hash mark we could hear Don calling the play on fruit instead of the hut-two cadence as a self-preservation measure.

He said, "Apples! Oranges! Bananas!" We always snapped the ball on the word *peaches*.

Well, this just broke up the Steelers' defense, and we could hear them laughing at Meredith.

For the rest of the game they took it pretty easy on Don. They would just knock him down to the ground rather than trying to annihilate him. Somehow he got them to see him more like a stand-up comic than the enemy.

When Ernie Stautner came to the Cowboys in 1965 as an assistant coach, I asked him why the defense started to take it easy on Meredith.

He said, "Did you hear him calling the play on fruit?"

I said, "Yeah, I did."

Ernie replied, "Well, that told us that he had had enough, so we quit beating up on him and never did it again for the remainder of the game."

In 1965 we drafted Craig Morton out of the University of California and Jerry Rhome from Tulsa. Jerry and Craig were both quarterbacks, and Meredith jokingly said, "I don't guess he [Coach Landry] thinks a whole lot of me."

Don was a great guy. But he played at a time when we were a struggling team and he really got beat up. Meredith had the capabilities to be an outstanding quarterback and to have his name listed up there with the greats, such as Montana, Elway, Staubach, and Bradshaw. He met all the criteria that it took to be in that select group of men. He just didn't have a good enough offensive line to protect him during the early years.

The year 1967 turned out to be a season of injuries for Don. The fact that he even played in the Ice Bowl was a testament to his toughness.

First, he broke a rib against Baltimore in the final preseason game. The following week, he beat the Browns at Cleveland for the first time ever and threw for 205 yards and two touchdowns. He continued to play three more games with fractured ribs and beat the Redskins with a last-second touchdown pass to Dan Reeves. When Don went to the hospital to have his ribs checked the following week, the doctors discovered that the reason he was feeling weak was because he had pneumonia.

After three weeks on the sideline, he returned to lead Dallas to a 37–7 win over the Falcons. Against Philadelphia, Don had his nose broken—something that he would experience 14 times throughout his career. Six days later against San Francisco—plastic face mask and all—he twisted his knee and was forced to come out of the game.

On Christmas Eve at the Cotton Bowl, a little over a week after he twisted his knee, Don beat the Cleveland Browns to send the Cowboys into the title game against the Packers.

Don was our quarterback of the future, a guy with a great arm and a wonderful personality. In the early days when Dallas was basically nobody's team, he was the bright spot—always laughing, clowning, and singing. But don't let that fool you. He was also a fierce competitor, and his goal was to win.

Not only was he smart and competitive, but he had a great sense of leadership. Meredith took us to two championship playoff games when the team really wasn't that good. He was definitely a man ahead of his time.

In 1968 we were in a playoff game against the Cleveland Browns. Meredith had been hospitalized with injuries that were suffered in a previous game. He obviously wasn't in the lineup. Don's loyalty to the team was so heartfelt that he left the hospital with a broken rib, a punctured lung, and pneumonia to play in the game and help out his team—only to suffer abuse from the media about his performance. (We lost the game.) For a person as courageous as Don to leave the hospital, risk his own health for his team, and then be blamed for the team's loss is absolutely appalling!

That's when Meredith quit football and never returned to the game as a player. After playing nine years with the Cowboys, Don retired in the summer of 1969 and went on to bigger and better things.

In September of 1970, Dandy Don cohosted *Monday Night Football* with Howard Cosell (the man everyone loved to hate) and Keith Jackson. Former New York Giants halfback and Hall of

Fame great Frank Gifford, who was the straight man of the three, replaced Jackson the following year. He was known for singing his signature song, "Turn Out the Lights, the Party's Over," when the winner of the game had long been decided.

Cosell and Meredith agreed to disagree while Gifford planned his play-by-play analogy. They would become *Monday Night Football's* first broadcast team and the greatest trio ever.

Sometimes Meredith would say some critical things about Coach and crack a few jokes about him. One time he compared Coach to the then Minnesota coach, Bud Grant. In front of a national television audience, Don said, "In a personality contest between Tom Landry and Bud Grant, there would be no winner."

In 1976 Don was inducted into the Ring of Honor, and in 2007 he received the Pro Football Hall of Fame's Pete Rozelle Radio-Television Award. Don's presenter of the award was his former *Monday Night Football* broadcasting partner and friend, Frank Gifford.

20

Players Year by Year

The Class of 1961

Chuck Howley

Chuck was starting over. He was traded to the Cowboys in '61, so he and I basically were rookies together.

Chuck was one of the finest defensive players in the history of the Dallas franchise. He was a five-sport letterman at West Virginia University and had been the number one draft choice of the Bears in 1958. In 1959 he injured his knee and retired from football to manage a service station in West Virginia.

But the Cowboys' Tex Schramm had heard about Chuck through one of Howley's former Bears teammates. Don Healy, who went to the Cowboys in the expansion draft, was a defensive tackle who had played with Chuck under George Halas. He told Tex that Chuck was interested in returning to professional football.

In 1961 Tex made a deal with the Bears and acquired the 6′4″, 235-pound outside linebacker. He and I played our rookie seasons together.

Chuck was known to his teammates as "Hogmeat." He was extremely agile and played the game with intelligence, skill, and instinct.

Chuck played 13 years for the Cowboys (1961–1973), was the MVP in Super Bowl V (intercepting two passes and recovering a fumble in the Cowboys' 16–13 loss to the Colts), and was All-Pro six times during his career. In 1977 I had the honor of presenting Chuck as he was inducted into the Ring of Honor. He was only the fourth player to have received that honor at that time.

The Class of 1962

George Andrie
When rookie defensive end George Andrie showed up at training camp, he was long on hope and short on experience. At 6′7″ and 250 pounds, George was the sixth-round draft choice of the Cowboys even though his school, Marquette University, had dropped the football program in his senior year.

George spent the majority of his career playing alongside me. He was so concerned about his caliber of play after losing a year at Marquette that he vowed never to miss a practice—not even when his leg was infected with gangrene!

We became very close friends and roomed together for 10 years. George was one of those players who made the big plays.

George was one of those players who made the big plays.

Two that I remember well are when he recovered a fumble and ran it in for a touchdown in the1967 Ice Bowl at Green Bay and when he intercepted a swing pass and scored against San Francisco in the conference playoffs—the same year we won the Super Bowl.

George played the flex defense like nobody else could and was extremely instrumental in building our Doomsday Defense. Even at 6′7″, he was still able to get low enough to stop blockers from getting under him. When closing a trap play,

George would hit his opponents with such force that his shoulder pads sounded like cannons firing.

ANDRIE'S STORY

One night some of the guys and I had a little get-together in my room. The main topic of discussion had to do with our financial woes.

After listening to us complain, Mike Gaechter challenged my roommate, George Andrie, to a dare. He said, "George, if you are in need of money, I will pay you twenty dollars to jump out of that window!"

Even though we were on the third floor of the building, it didn't look that high up because there was a big green awning below us that looked like grass.

George took Mike up on his offer and climbed through the window, hung on the sill, and then released his grip. Not only did we see George fall onto the awning, but we heard a ripping sound as his body went through it. Lucky for him, he landed in the hedges below.

At that moment Tex Schramm and Gil Brandt walked out of a nearby restaurant. They stood there and talked for a while as George lay there silently. At this point I wasn't even sure if he was even still alive.

The guys left, and I was there alone wondering what I would say to Coach Landry if George was seriously hurt, or worse, dead.

Soon I heard a knock at the door. It was George! As he entered the room I noticed blood dripping from the scratches on his arms and face caused by the stickers and sharp thorns in the hedges.

I said, "Oh, my goodness, George. Are you okay?"

All he said was, "Where's my money? I want my twenty bucks!"

I didn't know what to say to George, and Mike was nowhere to be found, so I went to each of the guys' rooms and collected about sixteen dollars—most of which was change.

I guess George was satisfied with the amount, because he didn't throw me out of the window! We still laugh about that night and have remained friends to this day.

Don Talbert

Don had an unusual career playing offensive tackle for the Cowboys. He joined us as a rookie in '62 and then spent two years in the army. He returned in '65 as the first Vietnam War veteran in the NFL and played a season before moving on to new expansion teams in Atlanta and New Orleans. He became a Cowboy again in '71—our first Super Bowl championship season.

Don didn't have a lot of natural ability, but he had great determination and was always giving a word of encouragement. He was a tough cookie and the oldest of three Talbert brothers who starred at the University of Texas. The youngest, Diron, later became a big Cowboys nemesis with the Redskins.

Don was very loyal to his alma mater. Once he and Pete Gent shared an apartment and Bobby Layne, the great old pro and Longhorns quarterback, came by for some drinks after Texas beat Oklahoma.

After a while Don put his arms upon Layne's shoulders and said, "Bobby, how 'bout those Horns?" Layne looked at Don and said, "Bleep the Horns!" Talbert was shocked, but Pete started laughing. Don wasn't about to do anything physical to Bobby Layne, whom he idolized, so instead he hit Pete in the stomach. Pete said he stayed on the floor for half an hour, and Don stepped on him every time he went to the bar to fix Bobby a drink.

Dave Edwards

Dave became one of the mainstays of our defense after he won a job as strong-side linebacker, but he almost didn't stay long enough to prove himself. He spent his rookie season in '63 on the taxi squad—probably making less pay than he did in training camp—and he shared an apartment with George Andrie and Mike Gaechter. They got a little wild at a party one night and the manager complained to Coach Landry about them throwing bottles in the swimming pool. Coach was so hot that he was ready to kick them all off. But some of us talked to him, and he decided to put them on probation and fine them. Once Dave survived that, he became a solid linebacker. He wasn't fast, but he was very strong. He just chucked those tight ends so they could hardly get off the ball. He never had much publicity, but he was highly respected by opponents. They just couldn't run against him.

Mike Gaechter

Mike, like George Andrie, made a good first impression as a player. Signed by Gil Brandt and Tex Schramm, Mike came to the Cowboys as a free agent because of his athletic ability in track. In 1962 Gaechter, with Oregon teammates Mel Renfro, Jerry Tarr, and Harry Jerome, set a world record in the 440-yard relay.

He had a wiry build and was very fast—he had been a sprinter at the University of Oregon who played a little football. He and Dave Edwards enjoyed being flamboyant bachelors with their cool clothes and sunglasses, but Mike was more than just flash on the football field. He became a very good, tough-hitting strong safety. In one of his first games as a rookie he intercepted a Philadelphia pass and ran 100 yards for a touchdown. That's still a club record.

At times, Mike could also act a lot like John Wilbur—very blunt and violent. He was a hard-nosed athlete, and when he hit somebody, he meant it. In dealing with people Mike never minced words.

He and I became good friends during the eight seasons he played defensive back. He was a very complex, very bright person.

A torn Achilles tendon probably took three or four years off his playing career, and I think that may have soured Mike on the Cowboys. Later he filed a lawsuit against the team doctor and the club because he believed they were responsible for shortening his career.

Mike stood up for himself, but he was also sensitive and caring toward others. He never was an easy guy to understand, but I've always liked him.

Cornell Green

At 6′3″ and 205 pounds, Cornell Green gave the Cowboys far more than anyone expected when he reported as a rookie in '62. He came to us from Utah State University, where he didn't play football but instead was a three-time All–Skyline Conference basketball player. Cornell played 13 years as a defensive back, was a four-time All-Pro, and played in five Pro Bowls. He was the brother of Pumpsie Green, the first African American player to play for the Boston Red Sox, the last team to integrate.

Tex Schramm had a theory about athletes. If an athlete had size and enough ability, he could learn to play the game of football.

Coach Landry couldn't have agreed more. He once said this about Cornell: "He had the athletic skills from basketball to become a fine defensive back. His only transition was playing a sport where you could tackle someone with the ball, and Cornell never had a problem dealing with that."

Green had the ability to play every position in the secondary, but due to his lack of football experience during the first day at training camp, Cornell put his hip pads on backward. He thought the part that covered your tailbone was supposed to protect the male organ. By the end of the day, his skin was torn up from wearing the pads incorrectly.

I will always remember two things about Cornell. First, for a person who had played as much basketball as he did, he had terrible hands for catching a football. We called him "Boards." Cornell could have had many more interceptions if only he had held onto the ball.

Second, he had a wonderful sense of humor and kept us laughing all the time. Calvin Hill, who was hurt a lot throughout his career, came into the locker room one day asking if anyone wanted his dog. Calvin's wife had asked him to find the dog a new home. Cornell said that he might take the dog, but he was afraid to…because, like Calvin, the dog might be prone to injury.

He had a wonderful sense of humor and kept us laughing all the time.

Cornell Green retired in 1974 and went on to become a scout with the Cowboys and later with the Denver Broncos.

Pettis Norman

Pettis Norman was another unknown rookie in '62, and broadcasters tended to say his name backward. But there was nothing backward about his style of play.

Pettis, unlike Frank Clarke and Don Perkins, grew up in the Deep South where the Jim Crow laws were still in effect. He was determined to never let anyone or anything defeat him. His morals as well as his sense of righteousness helped him to be successful both on and off the football field.

Norman was an All-American offensive end whom the Cowboys signed as a free agent out of Johnson C. Smith University near Charlotte, North Carolina. Dallas immediately converted him to a tight end.

A tremendous competitor, Pettis Norman was one of the best blocking tight ends I ever saw. He played with the Cowboys from 1962 to 1970.

Sam Baker

We had a real character on our team by the name of Sam Baker. Sam was the kicker for the Cowboys. He used to get under Coach's skin all the time.

One time during training camp, Sam refused to run what was known as "the Landry Mile." When Coach confronted him about the situation, Sam pulled out a letter that he had received prior to camp. It stated that "all linemen and backs will be timed in the mile run at the beginning of camp." According to Sam, it said nothing about kickers having to run the mile.

Coach finally talked him into doing the task. Still belligerent, Sam decided to run only the straights of the field and walk the curves. Coach just shook his head.

The other funny thing Sam did happened during a team meeting. Coach was in the middle of telling the team that they weren't in harmony and needed to pull together more. All of a sudden a humming sound was heard throughout the room. Sam was trying to get the team "harmonized" by starting them off in the right key.

The final straw came after a preseason game in Cleveland. Sam somehow missed the Cowboys' charter flight back to training camp and had to catch the only commercial flight available later that evening.

He finally arrived at the facility at 4:00 AM. Sam proceeded to knock on Coach's door and let him know that he had made it back. Half asleep, Coach Landry opened the door. Sam instantly came to attention, clicked his heels, saluted, and proclaimed, "Baker reporting for duty, sir!"

Coach immediately fined him $1,000 for missing the flight, slammed the door, and traded him the following season.

A few years later, Landry was named coach of the Pro Bowl. He and his assistant Dick Nolan spent some time gathering players' names to compose the special-teams unit. When Tom asked Dick to choose the best kicker for the Pro Bowl team, Dick responded, "It's Sam Baker." Tom quickly responded, "Okay, who's the second best?"

Sonny Gibbs

Sonny came from TCU a couple of years after I joined the Cowboys. He looked like he just might make it as a quarterback. He was 6'8" with a tremendously strong arm, and I was thrilled when the coaches made him their top draft choice.

Sonny lived in Graham, Texas—about 30 miles from my hometown of Throckmorton—and we were very good friends. In college we visited each other a lot and went hunting and fishing.

He and Don Meredith—both being quarterbacks—became very close. Sonny copied Meredith's lifestyle: a flamboyant playboy. But there was one difference between them. Meredith could afford to go out and party because he was a great quarterback, and he knew and understood the Cowboys' system. Sonny, on the other hand, had no experience, threw erratically, and just couldn't keep up with Don. The Cowboys had just acquired Pete Gent, and in order to keep him on the team Sonny was released after playing only one year.

Lee Folkins

Lee was a man with a great sense of humor. He was a 6′5″, 215-pound talented tight end who played three seasons with the Cowboys (1962–1964). He came to the Cowboys in '62 after an unusual career with the Green Bay Packers.

As a rookie in '61, Lee played on Vince Lombardi's first championship team. In August of '62 he was playing against the College All-Stars when he accidentally knocked out an official.

After he was traded to Pittsburgh in '65, he came back to play against us in the Cotton Bowl. Late in the game the Steelers scored, but we still led by a couple of touchdowns. On the ensuing kickoff, Lee ran downfield. When one of our receivers fumbled the ball, Lee recovered it on a bounce and ran into the end zone for a touchdown. He continued running and made a large circle in front of our bench. When he arrived in front of where Coach Landry had been standing, he tossed him the ball and kept going.

Class of 1963

Lee Roy Jordan

If you had to fight a war you would want Lee Roy Jordan on your side. He would never give up. He was extremely intense on the field and a tough competitor with tremendous self-confidence. Lee Roy was a student of the game, and he played the game hard and played it well.

A number one draft choice out of Alabama who played under Coach Bear Bryant, Jordan was somewhat small for his position as middle linebacker. At 6′1″ and 215 pounds, his competitiveness and drive made up for his lack in stature. Bear Bryant called him the best football player he ever coached. Pound for pound, I have no doubt that Coach Bryant was right.

Ralph Neely (No. 73) reported to the Cowboys as a rookie in 1965. At 6´6˝ and 275 pounds, the rookie became a big part of our offensive line. When I met Neely, I knew right away that he would become an All-Pro offensive tackle. George Andrie (No. 66) was a 6´7˝, 250-pound rookie from Marquette University. As a defensive end he played the flex defense like nobody else could. We became very close friends and roomed together for 10 years. PHOTO COURTESY OF BOB LILLY

Dan Reeves was just 20 years old when he came in as a rookie in 1965. He was an intense competitor and one of the true students of the game. He knew each and every player's assignment on each and every play. Coach Landry eventually made him a player-coach. PHOTO COURTESY OF BOB LILLY

Bob Hayes came to the Cowboys in 1965. He was an Olympic gold-medal sprinter who became an exciting star receiver for the Cowboys and was once considered the world's fastest man. Hayes and Don Meredith had some great games together, and they created an excitement that led to the Cowboys being named "America's Team."
PHOTO COURTESY OF BOB LILLY

Walt Garrison was the Cowboys' cowboy. When the fullback signed as a rookie in 1966, he asked for a two-horse trailer as a bonus. Walt could run and catch and was so tough that he played an entire playoff game against San Francisco with a broken collarbone. He dipped a lot of snuff, was a masterful whittler, and told us all the great stories of the rodeo. We got a lot more than a fullback when we got Walt. PHOTO COURTESY OF BOB LILLY

D.D. Lewis always had an easy smile, even when he had his bridge out. A promising rookie linebacker in 1968, D.D. played 12 years for Dallas. He wasn't very big, but he could hit with an incredible knockout power. Although he was never really hurt too bad, ol' D.D. seemed to have better luck with his body than he did with his teeth. PHOTO COURTESY OF BOB LILLY

Calvin Hill was the Cowboys' first draft choice in 1969. Out of Yale, this 6′4″, 230-pound halfback made All-Pro and Rookie of the Year—something no one expected from a guy who played in the Ivy League Conference. In 1972 he became the club's first 1,000-yard rusher. PHOTO COURTESY OF BOB LILLY

Roger Staubach reported to the Cowboys in 1969. Don Meredith had just retired, and Craig Morton became the starting quarterback. But Roger was never satisfied with being a backup; he was a natural leader with a strong competitive edge. He thrived on a challenge and loved to battle back and win. It's no surprise, then, that Roger became the starting quarterback in 1971 and led us to victory in Super Bowl VI.
PHOTO COURTESY OF BOB LILLY

A few of the Doomsday Defense players. From left to right: Willie Townes (No. 71), Jethro Pugh (No. 75), me (No. 74), and George Andrie (No. 66). PHOTO COURTESY OF THE DALLAS COWBOYS

From left to right: George Andrie, Tony Liscio, Ron East, and Blaine Nye.
PHOTO COURTESY OF BOB LILLY

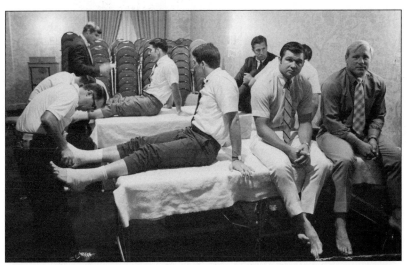

Neckties, dress shirts, and bare feet were standard on the morning of a game. Trainers taped most of the players at the hotel before the game. Here, Chuck Howley is being taped while Mike Ditka and Dave Manders wait for their turns. PHOTO COURTESY OF BOB LILLY

The frozen tundra at Lambeau Field. The 1967 championship game, also known as "the Ice Bowl," saw temperatures drop as low as 16 degrees below zero. The Packers beat us 21–17. PHOTO COURTESY OF BOB LILLY

When we arrived in Green Bay for the 1967 championship game, the temperature was in the low 20s with light snow. Don Meredith cupped his hands and said, "Easy money, baby. Easy money." Lance Rentzel and Bob Hayes agreed with him. PHOTO COURTESY OF BOB LILLY

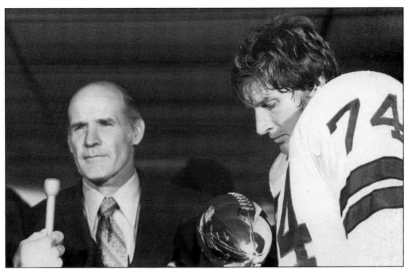

January 16, 1972, at Tulane Stadium in New Orleans, Louisiana. Coach Landry and me with the Lombardi Trophy after defeating Miami 24–3 and winning Super Bowl VI. PHOTO COURTESY OF THE DALLAS COWBOYS

In the 1972 Pro Bowl the Dallas Cowboys were represented by eight players. From left to right: Rayfield Wright, Chuck Howley, John Niland, me, Roger Staubach, Mel Renfro, Cornell Green, and Rod Widby. PHOTO COURTESY OF THE DALLAS COWBOYS

Pro Football Hall of Fame induction ceremony in Canton, Ohio, on August 2,1980. Coach Landry left training camp in California and flew all night to present me. It was a wonderful thing for him to do, and it was typical of the kind of man he was. He always had class. PHOTO COURTESY OF THE PRO FOOTBALL HALL OF FAME

The Doomsday Defense 40 years later. From left to right: George Andrie, me, Lee Roy Jordan, Jethro Pugh, and Larry Cole. PHOTO COURTESY OF THE DALLAS COWBOYS

His first year with the Cowboys, Lee Roy injured his foot playing the outside linebacker position. After having surgery on the arch of his foot, he hobbled into camp the following year, and through sheer guts he worked himself back into top playing condition.

Over the years he had built himself up to 221 pounds, but it was his commitment, determination, and knowledge of the game that made him better than many middle linebackers weighing 230 pounds or better.

If you had to fight a war you would want Lee Roy Jordan on your side.

Lee Roy and I had a code that we used during a game. If he noticed that the center was leaning my way and was going to cut me off, he would say, "Bob." If the center leaned the other way, he would say "Jethro."

Lee Roy consistently and meticulously watched game films and memorized computer printouts so he would be able to spot any changes during a game. If a running back leaned or cheated in his stance, Lee Roy saw it.

He became the franchise's all-time leader in solo tackles (743) in his 14 seasons with the Cowboys. He was a two-time All-Pro and a five-time Pro Bowl player. He also helped the Cowboys to three Super Bowls and five NFC Championship Games.

In 1989 he became the seventh member to be inducted into the Ring of Honor.

Tony Liscio

One of the nicest things Vince Lombardi ever did for us was releasing Tony Liscio. He was a big, promising offensive tackle and a high draft choice, but the Packers didn't have a place for him, so the Cowboys picked him up at the end of training camp in 1963.

At 6'5" and 260 pounds, Tony was a starter for the Cowboys for the next eight years. He was blessed with great balance and natural strength—and boy, could he eat!

Tony was born into a large Italian family in Pittsburgh, Pennsylvania. When the Cowboys played the Steelers, Coach Landry would do anything he could to keep Tony from dining at his mom's house, but he loved nothing more than to come home to his mother's great Italian cooking…and that's where the problem began. After consuming more than a few meals at his mom's house, Tony would return to the Cowboys five or ten pounds heavier!

Tony first announced that his retirement would begin in 1971, but at the request of Coach Landry, he returned to the Cowboys for the second half of the '71 season. Our tackle Ralph Neely had broken his leg in a motorcycle accident, and we needed Tony to replace him in Super Bowl VI.

After the Cowboys won the Super Bowl, Tony officially retired in January 1972.

Larry Stephens

Larry was probably one of the brightest players on our team. He seemed to pick up Landry's system better and faster than any other player.

In 1960 Larry was drafted by the Cleveland Browns. He played two years with the Browns, and his only NFL touchdown came on a 34-yard interception return, ironically against the Cowboys.

In 1962 he was traded to the Rams and was a defensive tackle alongside Merlin Olsen, Lamar Lundy, and Deacon Jones. Not bad, huh?

In 1963 he was traded to us and became a part of our Doomsday Defense until a knee injury slowed him down in 1966.

Larry was a big part of the Cowboys—from our humble beginnings to becoming championship contenders. Larry passed away in 1998.

Harold Hays

Harold Hays was a good backup linebacker, captain of our special teams, and the best fisherman I've ever seen, but what he wanted most was to be a starter for the Cowboys.

After five years with the team he was frustrated because his dream had never become a reality. He asked Coach to trade him at the end of the 1967 season. Assistant coach Dick Nolan, who had just left our staff to become the head coach of the 49ers, brought Harold to San Francisco with him.

Harold played with the 49ers for only two years before leaving the NFL for good.

Jim Ray Smith

Jim was a native-born Texan who wanted to live year-round in Dallas for two reasons. First, he wanted to live in the same city where he played football, and second, he wanted to continue to build his prosperous real-estate business.

From 1956 to 1962, he was an All-Pro guard for the Cleveland Browns, helped the team lead the league in rushing in 1958 and 1959, and was selected to five Pro Bowls before he finished his career with the Cowboys in '63 and '64.

He came from a winning team and gave us confidence in our ability to excel. He was honest and a hard worker, and I feel that the Cowboys benefited from his work ethic.

Dave Edwards

At 6'1" and 235 pounds, Dave was drafted by the AFL Denver Broncos in 1962 but decided to sign with the Cowboys as a free agent in 1963.

Dave became one of the Dallas mainstays on our defense after he won the job as strong-side linebacker in 1965, but he almost didn't stay long enough to prove himself.

His rookie season was spent on the taxi squad, and he shared an apartment with George Andrie and Mike Gaechter. One night they all got a little wild at a party and began throwing beer bottles into the swimming pool. The manager complained to Coach Landry about their actions. Tom was so mad that he was ready to kick them all off the team! A few of the other players and I were able to convince Coach to keep them. Dave, George, and Mike were all put on probation and fined heavily. After that, Dave manned the strong-side linebacker position and helped anchor the Doomsday Defense for 11 seasons. He was highly respected among his opponents.

On December 12, 1970, Dave intercepted two passes against Cleveland, helping the Cowboys earn a 6–2 victory that sent us into the playoffs.

Coach Stautner spoke highly of Dave when he said, "The best thing you can say about Edwards is that he's a pro. He plays while he's hurt and he still does an outstanding job. That's what a pro is."

Dave retired after the 1975 season.

Class of 1964

Dave Manders

At our Michigan training camp in 1962, Dave looked good as a center, but before we headed back to Texas he had been cut from the team. He later got married, completed his engineering degree, got a job, and played minor league football for two seasons.

In 1964, our training camp had been moved to Thousand Oaks, California. Dave returned to the Cowboys as a walk-on and made the team.

By 1966 he had replaced Mike Connelly as the starting center and made the Pro Bowl. He was a lot bigger than Mike—about 255 pounds with big, powerful legs. If he was knocked down during a game and saw a rusher going for the quarterback, he would leg-whip him—which was legal in those days. The rusher would wind up on the ground next to Dave. He retired along with me in 1974.

Mel Renfro

Mel was a two-way Oregon Ducks star when the Cowboys were interested in drafting him, but he had severely cut the nerves and tendons of his hand when he punched a mirror—reacting to the news that President Kennedy had been assassinated. The injury caused him to lose feeling in some of his fingers. It kept him out of the "Civil War" game against Oregon State and the Ducks' Sun Bowl win over Southern Methodist—something that would come back to haunt him.

Back in the '60s, scouting was a combination of luck, skill, and a bit of unorthodox behavior. Gil Brandt wanted to draft Mel but knew that his injury and the fact that he missed his last two college games would keep him from becoming a first-round draft choice.

Just prior to the '64 draft, Brandt and the Cowboys began spreading rumors regarding the seriousness of Mel's injury. They told the rest of the league that it was far worse than it really was. But on draft day, word got out that Mel would be taken in the first round by Dallas.

Dallas held up the draft for several hours by trying to negotiate a trade with Pittsburgh's Buddy Parker for wide receiver Buddy Dial. Everyone thought that Dallas was wheeling and dealing for Mel. To their surprise, Scott Appleton was drafted in the first round—not Renfro—making the other teams believe that they found a problem with the Ducks' running back; therefore, no one else drafted him in the first round.

Everyone thought that Dallas was wheeling and dealing for Mel.

When it was the Cowboys' second turn in the draft, they immediately took Mel in the second round. The reaction? The other teams cried out that they had been taken for a ride. Oh, the trials and tribulations of NFL draft day.

I personally was delighted when the Cowboys chose Mel. Not only was he a great running back but he was also a natural athlete—a phenomenal sprinter and hurdler in track. Mel was a part of the 1962 440-yard relay team that set a world record with a time of 40.0 seconds. One of his track teammates was future Cowboys teammate Mike Gaechter.

Mel initially played safety but was switched to the cornerback position in 1969. His skill and athleticism at his new position made him a threat to wide receivers. He was selected to the Pro Bowl every year for his first 10 seasons, and he made All-Pro five times. In 1981 I had the honor of welcoming Mel into the Ring of Honor. In 1996 his greatness on the gridiron was finally recognized when he was inducted into the Hall of Fame.

Jim Colvin

Jim came to us in a trade with the Baltimore Colts. He played opposite me at the left tackle position. He had a great sense of humor and was very upbeat—just what the team needed to help boost our confidence.

Jim always commented on how great our team was and the high caliber of talented players that made up the Dallas Cowboys. He motivated and inspired us at a time when we didn't think very highly of ourselves.

He also knew how to take the drudgery out of training camp. When Jim arrived at the dorm, the first thing he did was rent a bed, a TV, and a refrigerator. Then he taped black plastic sheets over his windows. Once settled in, it was just like home sweet home.

Pete Gent

Pete was the second basketball player to win a job with the Cowboys. He wasn't drafted but took a chance and showed up at the Dallas training camp in the summer of '64. He had heard that the Cowboys were offering $500 to players who attended their camp.

Pete made the team and played wide receiver and tight end from 1964 to 1968—deciding to turn down a pro basketball offer upon leaving Michigan State.

Pete had great hands and played tough. Toward the end of his Cowboys career his knee began to break down, but he hung in there and played as well as he could.

He was bright, humorous, and at times extremely sarcastic. He was always mouthing off before games. Once, before a big game in St. Louis, Pete called Larry Wilson (the Cardinals' All-Pro free safety) the ugliest man he'd ever seen. Wilson really pounded him in that game, but Pete still caught the ball in the clutch.

One time, before our next game with the Eagles, Coach Landry decided he was going to play Pete at the split end position instead of flanker.

He said to Pete, "You're going to play on the other side next week."

Pete just looked at him and asked, "I'm going to play for Philadelphia?"

Gent may have been disenchanted with football and the Cowboys, but he still could make me laugh. When he was a rookie he said, "I didn't know what a free agent was until I got my first paycheck."

In 1969 Dallas traded Pete to the New York Giants, but he never played for them.

In 1973, a few years after his final season with Dallas, Pete wrote a semiautobiographical novel entitled *North Dallas Forty*. All the names were changed, but Pete had obviously developed his plot and characters from his experiences with the Cowboys and the NFL. His story was purely fictional, of course, but it reflected the attitude Pete had when he was a Cowboy.

Many of us felt that the main characters of the book, the quarterback and his receiver, were based on real-life Dallas players Don Meredith and Pete Gent. In my opinion, much of what he said about us was exaggerated; we weren't that bad!

> *The book emphasized the dark side of football*

The book emphasized the dark side of football—life in the fast lane and the reckless use of painkillers. In 1979 the book was made into a movie (of the same name) with Pete writing the screenplay. *North Dallas Forty* starred Mac Davis as Seth Maxwell, the team's flamboyant quarterback, and Nick Nolte as Phil Elliott, his receiver and best friend, who was dependant upon painkillers in order to continue to play the game.

Jim Boeke

Jim was a big ole boy—6′6″ or so—and a pretty good offensive lineman for us in the '60s. He came to us in a Les Josephson trade with the Rams.

I remember Jim as a great competitor and a tremendous wit. I still see him occasionally in movie bit parts and TV commercials.

Buddy Dial

If ever a guy came to the Cowboys with great dreams and expectations, it was Buddy. He was an All-American end at Rice and had a great career with Pittsburgh, but he always dreamed of one day returning to his home state of Texas.

In 1964 Don Meredith found a favorite receiver and good friend in Buddy Dial. Like Meredith, he was not a Landry disciple. Buddy was worse: he was a Bobby Layne disciple!

While with the Steelers, Buddy was Bobby's primary receiver and primary partier. When Coach Landry traded for Buddy the receiver, he also inherited a country western singer who loved to cruise the bars and sing with honky-tonk women.

When Buddy arrived at training camp he was completely out of shape. The Landry Mile and the 40-yard dash were completely out of the question.

One day nearing the end of practice, Meredith wanted to run just one more play. He told Buddy to run long down the sideline. Buddy did just that, but in order to catch Meredith's pass, he had to jump and extend his upper body. As he leaped into the air, Buddy heard and felt his thigh muscle snap. The muscle had pulled away from the knee and Buddy required immediate surgery.

When the doctors reattached the muscle to the knee, they attached it too tightly. Buddy returned to his workout regimen only to have the muscle pull off the hip.

Buddy's playing days were now numbered, but while he was on injured reserve he played guitar, sang for the guys, and was a lot of fun to be with. He even began to record songs professionally.

He had one of the best personalities I've ever seen and began wheeling and dealing in a number of businesses. But when his injuries began to really bother him, his football career became just a memory.

Buddy began taking pills to kill the pain and became addicted to them. This led to major health problems brought on by abusing the drugs. Buddy was finally treated for his problem in the late 1980s.

He was such a great guy and a real go-getter. I truly believe that if he hadn't become addicted to the pills, he might have ended up owning all of New York City.

Maury Youmans
Maury was a defensive end who was drafted by the Bears back in 1959. After suffering a knee injury in a game with the Redskins, Maury missed the 1963 season and the championship game against the Giants that the Bears won. To add insult to injury, the MVP of the game was Maury's replacement.

Soon after, Maury received a call from Jim Ringo, his teammate at Syracuse, telling him that Vince Lombardi liked the way he played and wanted him to play for Green Bay. With that, Maury asked George Halas to trade him—and Halas did just that. But he traded him to Dallas.

Maury said that when he arrived at training camp in Thousand Oaks it was like Sunday school in comparison to the Bears' training camp. He couldn't get over how nice the guys were.

But Coach Landry's practices were a lot harder than the Bears'. Maury wasn't used to full pads and hitting all day. But he learned the flex defense very quickly and became a great player for the team.

Tommy McDonald

Tommy came to the Cowboys in a trade with the Philadelphia Eagles. He may have been short in stature, but he had a reputation for making the big plays. He was a first-class, All-Pro receiver who was a great asset to the Dallas team.

Not only did Tommy excel on the field, but he was also a very talented artist who painted beautiful portraits of the Cowboys players.

While at the University of Oklahoma he was coached by the great Bud Wilkinson and never played in a losing game. In 1956 he received the Maxwell Award and in 1955 and 1956 was an All-American.

In 1957 he was drafted by the Eagles and helped lead them to the 1960 NFL championship. Tommy led the league in touchdown receptions in both 1958 and 1961.

Tommy was also the last player to play in the NFL without a face mask (except kickers). Now that's what I call tough! He was inducted into the Pro Football Hall of Fame in 1998.

Class of 1965

Ralph Neely

Ralph played college ball for Bud Wilkinson at the University of Oklahoma and was an All-American in his senior year. He and two other Sooner players, one being future teammate Lance Rentzel, missed the 1965 Gator Bowl against Florida State because they signed on with agents before the game and were ruled ineligible to play.

When Ralph first reported as a rookie in 1965, I already knew that he would eventually become an All-Pro offensive tackle. He was extremely football oriented, and at 6′6″ and 265 pounds he became a big part of our offensive line. There was one problem. Ralph had first signed with Houston of the AFL, and the Oilers sued the Cowboys over claiming rights.

The Cowboys were finally able to keep Ralph, but only after going through a huge litigation and monetary settlement—including an agreement to play two exhibition games in Houston. In all, it cost the Cowboys about $750,000, but Ralph proved his worth to the organization.

Throughout his 13-year career with the Cowboys he was a two-time Pro Bowl player, was a five-time All-Pro, and was selected to the NFL's All-Time '60s Decade Team.

One thing about Ralph: he never hesitated to give the team his opinion. Dave Edwards appropriately nicknamed him "Mouther."

NEELY'S STORY

The term *relaxation* can mean many things to professional football players. To some it could be a relaxing day off; for others it could be an alternative form of unwinding—like dirt bikes!

The bikes weren't street legal—no license plates or head-lights—so we rode the country trails. We really had a lot of fun on those bikes, but Coach Landry didn't share our enthusiasm. He used to tell us, "Do what you want in the off hours, but you better not do anything to embarrass the team or hurt yourself, or you will be replaced."

There were several of us who rode: Dave Edwards, Ralph Neely, Charlie Waters, Cliff Harris, Walt Garrison, Dan Reeves, Mike Ditka, and myself. Some of the guys rode conservatively, but others, like Cliff Harris and Charlie Waters, rode their bikes fast and furious. Both went as far as to participate in motocross races under assumed names. Thank heavens Coach never caught them. But another member of our Dallas team, Ralph Neely, was not so lucky.

It was a beautiful Monday in January and our season was nearing its end. In two weeks we would be in New Orleans for Super Bowl VI. We all decided to meet at Lake Dallas to ride a series of trails that twisted and turned near the edge of the lake.

In order to ride the steep hills and narrow, sharp curves of the road, a rider must have the skill, ability, knowledge, and experience to know when to slow down and how to recognize danger, or he will find himself launched in midair.

Most of the guys rode bikes with engines that were around 250cc. Cliff Harris and Charlie Waters had 360 Yamahas, Dave Edwards drove a 400, and Ralph Neely had bought a brand-new 450 Kawasaki. That type of bike was for an experienced rider, which Ralph was not.

That particular day, Ralph experienced a bad day of falls. Each time he went down, we would all stop and wait for him to get up, curse his bike, and take off again.

At the end of the day, we returned to where we had parked our cars and trucks. Ralph wanted to go for one more run and had asked Cliff Harris to go with him. Cliff agreed. Their objective was to take a 300-yard-tall, grass-covered hill. Cliff, being the experienced rider, made it up the hill on his first try.

Ralph, on the other hand, made it about halfway up before he and his bike fell over. Furious and determined to make it up that hill, Ralph coasted back down, situated his bike so it was facing toward the hill, put it in second gear, and gunned it. His machine whined and screamed through the tall grass as he flew up the hill.

The combination of Ralph's inexperience as a rider and the power of the bike proved to be dangerous as Ralph hit the top of the hill and became airborne.

Instead of keeping his feet on the pegs, he extended his legs and tried to land on his feet. The outcome: a broken ankle.

I don't know what was worse, the broken ankle or having to tell Coach Landry what had happened. Either way, Ralph did not make the Super Bowl trip. Coach Landry brought former Cowboy Tony Liscio out of retirement to play Ralph's offensive tackle position in the Super Bowl, where we went on to beat Miami.

Not only did Tony get Ralph's Super Bowl check but he also got his Super Bowl ring!

Craig Morton

Craig was the number one draft choice of the Cowboys in 1965. He was an All-American at the University of California at Berkeley who came (along with Jerry Rhome from Tulsa) to be an understudy to Don Meredith. Even though he had two bad knees, he was still a very good quarterback. He helped us get to our first Super Bowl in 1970.

Craig was not known for his mobility on the field. He was strictly a downfield passer and had a tendency to throw the ball very hard. Pete Gent once said, "Craig Morton only threw at one speed—which was like shooting the ball out of a cannon!"

Once Craig threw a pass so hard that the force of the ball split Bob Hayes's hand in half. It took 17 stitches to close it up.

Craig would have probably had a much better chance of succeeding at the quarterback position if he had been brought in through a much smoother transition. When Don Meredith announced his retirement, it was a shock to everyone—including Craig.

Once Craig threw a pass so hard that the force of the ball split Bob Hayes's hand in half.

During training camp Craig should have been the number two quarterback, but instead he was forced into the starting position with a team that expected him to win. That was a tremendous request for a young quarterback.

Craig was an in-the-pocket passer who would hold his ground until he found a receiver or was sacked by the defense—whichever came first. The only problem was that Coach Landry's offensive strategies did not consider protecting the quarterback a high priority. The fact that Craig took his Dallas team as far as he did was a credit to his ability, his skill, and his loyalty to the ballclub.

In the end Craig's downfall was his lack of mobility, injuries, and his unfortunate timing to have played alongside an avid competitor such as Roger Staubach.

After the 1977 season, Craig led Denver all the way to Super Bowl XII, making him the only quarterback in NFL history to lead two different teams to the Super Bowl.

Jerry Rhome

Jerry Rhome came to us from the University of Tulsa, where he finished second in the 1964 Heisman Trophy voting. He played four seasons with the Cowboys and, like Craig Morton, was Don Meredith's understudy. At that time Coach Landry was rotating his quarterbacks, which was not very popular with the rest of the team.

Although Jerry was a dynamic quarterback, he realized that it would be many years before he would have a chance at the number one position.

In June 1969 Jerry demanded that Coach Landry trade him. His demand was acknowledged, and he was sent to the Cleveland Browns. He would later play for the Oilers and the Rams.

Following his retirement, Jerry became an assistant coach at his alma mater, the University of Tulsa, and later with the Seattle Seahawks.

Jethro Pugh

When the Cowboys said they had drafted Jethro Pugh from someplace called Elizabeth City State University in North Carolina, everybody asked, "What's a Jethro Pugh?" When he came to camp in 1965 we found out.

Jethro was knock-kneed with huge thighs and a very small waist. His chest and arms weren't that big so it made him look slender at 6′6″ and 260 pounds. But out on the field it was a different story. When Jethro put on his pads he had no trouble knocking guys around. He played opposite me at tackle, and we had a lot of fun in the middle.

Jethro was an outstanding tackle and played his entire 14-year career with the Cowboys. He was responsible for making many big plays, but in my opinion he never received the recognition he deserved.

PUGH'S STORY

Every day at 9:00 AM we would first have a team meeting with Coach Landry and then break off into our own offensive and defensive groups.

Next, Coach Stautner would meet with the entire defense, and then we would separate into our own squads—defensive backs with Coach Stallings, the defensive line with Coach Stautner, and the linebackers with Coach Tubbs.

One day, while the entire defensive team was present, Coach Stautner decided to talk us through one of his tedious analyses of a short-yardage play. As the monotony of his voice continued on and the sound of the projector softly whirled, I tried hard to keep my eyes open, but the dimly lit room had become incredibly warm and somewhat short on ventilation. Looking around, I noticed that some of the guys were asleep.

Suddenly the lights came on. It startled everyone—even some of the players who were asleep—well, all but one.

Sometime during Coach's tiresome monologue, Jethro Pugh had fallen asleep, and when his head fell back, it hit the light switch and turned on the lights. The only problem was that Jethro didn't wake up and continued to snore as the rest of us were hunching over with laughter. After practice, Coach saw to it that he ran a little more and a little farther than the rest of us.

Dan Reeves

Dan Reeves was just 21 years old when he came to the Cowboys as a rookie in 1965. While attending the University of South Carolina, Dan played the quarterback position. He came to the

Cowboys as a free agent and tried out as a running back. Dan spent eight seasons with the Cowboys, and over the years we became very good friends.

Most of us weren't real students of the game, but Dan knew every player's assignment on every play. He became a much better running back than anyone expected him to be. He wasn't fast, but he was deceptive and could limp-leg out of a tackle and get across the goal line.

The Cowboys made the playoffs every year of Reeves's playing days, reaching the Super Bowl twice and, in 1971, beating the Dolphins 24–3 in Super Bowl VI.

Right off the bat we nicknamed him "Red Reeves" because of his red hair and fiery temper. No matter whether he was playing cards, racquetball, or football or just throwing darts, he would be furious at himself if he didn't win. He was an intense competitor.

He and Mike Ditka used to play racquetball together after practice. Both were highly competitive and emotional, so when they got upset they would throw their racquets, often breaking them.

In need of replacement racquets, both Mike and Dan would go to the locker room and take someone else's racquet. We got wise to this and started locking up our racquets to prevent them from breaking ours as well.

Worn down by gridiron injuries, Dan became a player/coach in 1970, and after his retirement in 1972 he became the team's running backs coach. He went on to become Dallas's offensive coordinator in 1977, and in 1981, at age 37, Dan became head coach and vice president of the Denver Broncos. After a number of years at Denver, Dan went on to head coaching positions at the New York Giants and the Atlanta Falcons. In all, Dan was either a player or coach in nine Super Bowl games.

Bob Hayes

Bob was the most famous athlete the Cowboys ever signed. Earning the name "the World's Fastest Human," this gold medalist and 1964 Tokyo Olympics track champion came to us in 1965 and immediately became an exciting pass receiver. He gave the Cowboys and their fans a kind of speed and excitement that was unmatched by any other NFL team.

He gave the Cowboys and their fans a kind of speed and excitement that was unmatched by any other NFL team.

In his first year he caught passes for more than 1,000 yards and scored 12 touchdowns. Bob became the most dangerous deep threat in football.

He was the first player in the history of the Dallas franchise to exceed 1,000 yards receiving in a single season. Bob accomplished that in his rookie year by finishing with 1,003 yards. That same year, he led the team with 46 receptions and set franchise records with a total of 13 touchdowns and 12 receiving TDs.

Bob was at his best when racing free for long passes behind defensive backs who couldn't cover him man-to-man. But when NFL cornerbacks began using bump-and-run coverage and secondaries changed to zone defenses, Bob no longer enjoyed his natural advantage in one-on-one footraces. His role changed from hero to just another veteran wide receiver.

In 1975 his NFL career ended on a much quieter note than when he arrived 10 years earlier. When Bob found himself out of football it was a tough transition for him to make. He was a warm, outgoing guy, and I sensed he wanted very much to be needed and loved. A few years after his playing days had ended, Bob became heavily involved in the use of alcohol and narcotics.

On September 18, 2002, Bob died of kidney failure after battling prostate cancer and liver problems. He was only 59 years old.

Just prior to his death he told the *Dallas Morning News* his fondest memories of the 1964 Tokyo Olympics, saying, "I remember my mom with tears running down her face as they raised our flag. The emperor of Japan was crossing the track, our national anthem was playing, and the name on the billboard read 'Robert Hayes, USA.' And me thinking, 'I'm from the world's greatest country.'"

Some of my saddest and some of my warmest memories will always be of Bob Hayes. I truly miss him.

Danny Villanueva

Danny came to us from the Rams in 1965, and he was a pretty good punter and place-kicker. A combination like that was considered rare in the NFL, but after his second season, the Cowboys decided to look at other prospects.

In the spring of 1967 the Cowboys created the "Kicking Karavan." The organization sent some of their scouts across America and over to Europe to hold tryouts for kickers.

This completely enraged Danny. Even though the best prospects for the job tried out at camp, none of them could outkick Danny.

The next summer Dan waited until the day he was scheduled to report to training camp and then sent Coach Landry a telegram announcing his retirement. That left the Cowboys in a tough situation because they had to hustle around and trade for another kicker. Danny was a little vindictive, but maybe he had a right to be.

He settled down in Los Angeles and built a business empire in broadcasting, beer, and boxing. He promoted more than a dozen world championship fights and was named boxing commissioner for the 1984 Olympic Games.

Leon Donohue

Leon was an excellent guard during those first winning years, but when he hurt his knee it ended his career. When Leon was healthy, he was a great pass blocker and a positive person who lifted everyone's spirits.

Obert Logan

Nicknamed "Little O," Obert wasn't blessed with enough height or speed to be a star defensive back, but he was a great asset to the team in 1965 and 1966.

His jersey number was zero, and I believe he was the last football player to be assigned that number.

A true motivator, Little O was a positive influence on our team's spirit and confidence. It was a sad day for me when Obert passed away from cancer in 2003.

Malcolm Walker

Malcolm Walker was among the fine crop of rookies who were signed in 1965. There was no doubt that he would one day be a star on the Cowboys team, but like many other players, his career was cut short by a knee injury.

In 1968 Coach Landry moved Malcolm to the center position where he played as a backup for the next two years. In 1970 he was traded to the Green Bay Packers, where he ended his football career.

Class of 1966

John Niland

John came to the Cowboys from the University of Iowa, where he was an outstanding offensive guard. The Cowboys drafted him number one in 1966, and he was one of the best pulling guards I've ever seen. He was quick on the snap and would get to his man and knock him down, play after play after play. In practice, he stood directly in front of me, and I learned early on what an excellent player he really was.

John was flamboyant and enjoyed wearing expensive clothes and driving fancy cars, but on the field he was a great contributor to the team.

His career with the Cowboys lasted nine years. John was selected to six consecutive Pro Bowls and was an All-Pro. He was traded to the Philadelphia Eagles in 1975, played one season, and then retired.

Walt Garrison

Walt was the Cowboys' cowboy. A star fullback out of Oklahoma State, Walt signed with the Cowboys as a rookie in 1966. His signing bonus included a two-horse trailer.

He came in to play fullback and learned from the master, Don Perkins. Walt told me he didn't understand how Don could block as well as he did—because he never missed a block. But when Perk retired after the '68 season, Walt stepped into his position and blocked just as well as Don had.

Walt could both run and catch. He was so tough and so dependable that he once played an entire playoff game against San Francisco with a broken collarbone.

Walt was a real cowboy who worked the professional rodeo circuit in the off-season. He dipped a lot of snuff and was a long-time spokesperson for US Tobacco. He was also a masterful whittler and told us great stories about rodeo life. Some of us became his pupils of whittling, although none of us ever got as good at it as he is.

He was so tough and so dependable that he once played an entire playoff game against San Francisco with a broken collarbone.

He got his nickname "Puddin'" from Don Meredith, but I won't go into that. He was tough, intelligent, and entertaining, and he loved horses and rodeo as much as he did football. But his career in the NFL ended with a knee injury he suffered while bulldogging a steer. He came in a cowboy and went out a cowboy.

When quarterback Don Meredith was asked about Walt's dependability, Don humorously responded with, "If it was third down and you needed four yards, if you'd get the ball to Walt Garrison, he'd get ya five. And if was third down and ya needed twenty yards, if you'd get the ball to Walt Garrison, by God, he'd get you five."

John Wilbur

John played guard for the Cowboys for four years—1966 to 1969—and was always fiercely competitive and outspoken. He used to wear what he called a "rebellion hat"—something that Coach Landry didn't look highly upon.

John grew up in California and graduated from Stanford University at a time when the age of protest was reaching its peak. He was very intelligent as well as highly opinionated. There always was an underlying agitation with John.

He constantly was having ideological quarrels with other players about how the Cowboys organization operated, their political stance, the issue of race and prejudice among the coaches, and what they had to do with Dallas (as a Southern city).

John was a strange one. He was always getting into fights with defensive players in practice. I fought with him a lot myself. But during break period he'd come over and stand with us. He didn't associate much with offensive players, other than Pete Gent.

You could see how tough he was when he played on the kickoff team. John barreled downfield and tore up the blocking wedge like a wild man. Jim Myers, the offensive line coach, said, "John would challenge hell with a bucket of water!"

Willie Townes
Coach Landry had a standard fine for an overweight player—$25.00 per pound. I think Willie lost half of his salary that way. During training camp he had the distinction of sitting at the Fat Man's Table in the dining hall.

Willie was a really likeable guy and a pretty good defensive end when he joined us as a rookie in 1966, but he just couldn't keep his weight down.

One night around 11:30, George Andrie, Dave Edwards, Mike Gaechter, and I were talking when someone knocked on the window. I opened it up and a delivery boy handed me a great big pizza.

"This is for Willie," he said.

Well, we ate all but one-quarter of that pizza. Then I went across the hall and knocked on Willie's door. He opened the door, acting like he had been asleep.

I said, "Come on over, Willie. We have something for you."

We gave him the last of the pizza and told him, "Maybe you can lose weight on just a quarter of a pizza."

Willie also had a great appetite for life. He was a showman, a great salesman, and a very outgoing person. He was a clown—always doing something silly when I took his picture. But if he hadn't been so heavy, he would have had the ability to become a top defensive end. A leg injury handicapped him late in his career, but he basically ate his way out of the league.

He was a showman, a great salesman, and a very outgoing person.

Dick Daniels

Dickie Daniels was a fine little defensive back. He wasn't quite big enough to be a star, but he was very competitive, was very fast, and always did a good job on the kicking team.

Class of 1967

Lance Rentzel

Lance had already played a couple of years for the Minnesota Vikings when he joined us in 1967, and he quickly became a top receiver. The Cowboys didn't have to give up much in the trade, and at that time we didn't know he had had some problems off the field. All I saw then was a very bright young athlete who could run perfect routes, had great hands, and could catch the ball in a crowd.

He made some important plays for us, like catching a pass from halfback Dan Reeves for the touchdown that almost won Dallas the Ice Bowl.

He was an excellent pianist and entertained us a lot on the road. He'd find a piano in a hotel meeting room, and we would either sing along with him or just listen to him play. He added a little flair to our team in those days.

For all of his talents, he never seemed very happy. I look at all the pictures I've taken of him, and I see a hurt look in his eyes.

He'd find a piano in a hotel meeting room, and we would either sing along with him or just listen to him play.

He came from a wealthy family in Oklahoma, had a good football career, and married actress Joey Heatherton a couple of years after he joined the Cowboys. But in 1970 his life changed forever.

In November, just prior to our Thanksgiving Day game, Lance was arrested for indecent exposure. After that, Lance never played another down for the Cowboys. Coach Landry had him traded to the Los Angeles Rams.

In his book, *When All the Laughter Died in Sorrow,* Lance spoke of the resentment he felt over his release by the Cowboys and the damage to his reputation.

> *There were parts of it…like the hate mail. And the Rentzel jokes. I've heard them all. And it hurts, because as I've said many times, I feel like I have some good qualities, too. But when something like this happens, people only remember the bad things. I can't blame people. If that's all I had read, maybe I'd feel the same.*

In 1972 Lance wrote a book about his personal and professional football life entitled *When All the Laughter Died in Sorrow.*

Rayfield Wright

Rayfield was a 6′6″, 235-pound, All-American tight end and free safety when he was drafted from Fort Valley State College in Georgia. The Cowboys immediately employed him to the tight end position, but by the start of his third season his weight was up to 255 and he was moved to the offensive tackle position.

In November of 1969 we went to Los Angeles to play the Rams and Rayfield got his chance to start at left tackle after Ralph Neely had been sidelined with an injury.

Before the game someone had mentioned to Rayfield that playing against Deacon Jones, an All-Pro defensive end, was a tough way to break into the position.

Rayfield asked, "Why would that be tough?"

We told him that Deacon was big, tough, and very fast.

Rayfield replied, "I'm big, I'm tough, and I'm fast!"

His performance was so strong that he earned the starting role at left tackle and never looked back. He was All-Pro four times and named six times to the Pro Bowl.

In 2004 Rayfield was inducted into the Cowboys' Ring of Honor and in 2006, the Pro Football Hall of Fame.

Craig Baynham

Craig was drafted by the Cowboys out of Georgia Tech and was a big running back who possessed great speed. In the conference championship game against the Cleveland Browns on December 24, 1967, Craig scored three touchdowns to help the Cowboys achieve a 52–14 victory over the Browns at the Cotton Bowl.

He was an extremely religious person who would always include a written scripture with his autograph. He was a good influence on all of us.

His son Grant also played for Georgia Tech and was awarded the esteemed Robert Cup, given to Tech's top student athlete.

Ron East

Ron came to us from Montana State University. If he had been a little bigger, I'm sure he would have been a star at defensive tackle. He joined the Cowboys in 1967 and spent four years playing backup to Jethro Pugh and me.

He was a great guy who did a lot to keep our confidence up. Ron was always making fun of us or telling a joke, but he was also always a hundred percent on the field.

Class of 1968

D.D. Lewis
Dwight Douglas always had a big smile on his face, even when he had his bridge (teeth) out.

An All-American out of Mississippi State University, D.D. looked promising as a rookie linebacker in 1968, but he missed the 1969 season when he was called to active duty with the army. He came back ready to play in 1970 and spent 12 more years with the Cowboys.

He wasn't very big, but like Pettis Norman, D.D. exploded on the field. His hits were so powerful that he had the ability to knock you out. I'm sure that type of strength contributed to his long career. D.D. first served as a backup to Chuck Howley and later took over the weak-side linebacker position.

He always maintained that baby face and youthful image. He never got hurt. Ole D.D. had better luck with his body than he did with his teeth.

Larry Cole
Larry's slow-talkin', slow-walkin' image fooled a lot of people. It sure fooled the Cowboys, because they didn't draft him until the 16th round of the 1968 draft.

He really didn't impress anyone when he first wandered into camp. He played college football at the University of Hawaii,

Air Force, and Houston at both the defensive end and defensive tackle positions.

Larry not only made the team but played his entire 13-year career with Dallas. He was tough, dependable, and a big-play maker. In his last year with the Cowboys, he grabbed a deflected pass and ran it 43 yards for a touchdown.

Larry was a lot of fun to be around because he had a dry sense of humor. Many reporters interviewed Larry after games. One night a reporter mentioned that the last time he scored a touchdown was in 1969.

Larry just shrugged and said, "Anyone can have an off decade."

Blaine Nye

Blaine was drafted in the fifth round out of Stanford University. He played the guard position and was extremely intelligent. At 6´4″ and 250 pounds, Blaine was a big kid and very shy.

He and Larry Cole were very much alike. They mostly kept to themselves, did their own thing, and formed the Zero Club, which included those players who stayed out of the media's spotlight. They didn't get their names in the paper, they never were asked to make public appearances, and no one paid them to endorse or advertise anything.

Blaine and Larry were also alike on the field. They rarely made mistakes and were very aggressive. Blaine was very good at using his hands while he was pass blocking. He was so good that he rarely got caught by the refs. If he had gotten caught for holding, it would have been brought to the attention of the media, and he might have been kicked out of the Zero Club!

Blaine and Larry were also alike on the field. They rarely made mistakes and were very aggressive.

185

Mike Clark

At 6′1″ and 205 pounds, Mike Clark came to us from a trade with the Pittsburgh Steelers. He was a good kicker, but like all kickers, he had his share of bad days.

In our 1969 playoff game against the Browns at the Cotton Bowl, everything that could go wrong had gone wrong. It had rained all day, the field was a mess, and we had already blown the game when Mike tried an onside kick after we scored a late touchdown.

Mike ran up to the ball, did a little step, and then completely missed the ball and slipped down in the mud. I was sitting on the bench beside Dave Edwards. Dave had a knack for giving players nicknames. He yelled, "Way to go, Onside!" From that day on, Mike was known as "Onside."

Mike was diagnosed with advanced melanoma in 1998 and later passed away at Baylor University Medical Center after a fatal heart attack.

Ron Widby

Ron Widby was our punter when Mike Clark was our kicker, and he was a fine all-around athlete. He played college football and basketball at Tennessee and later played pro basketball with the New Orleans Buccaneers of the ABA. He also played pro golf and was an excellent tennis and racquetball player. He was selected to the Pro Bowl in 1971.

Ed Harmon

Ed was drafted by the Cowboys in the third round of the 1968 draft. He played on special teams and was a reserve linebacker who was known as a hard hitter with ferocious intensity.

186

Once he ran down under a kickoff and some guy hit him with an elbow. It broke his face mask and badly cut both his chin and lip. Ed wound up with 40 to 50 stitches in his face.

Class of 1969

Calvin Hill

In 1969 the first draft choice of the Cowboys was a halfback from Yale by the name of Calvin Hill. He was the first big back Dallas had had in years. At 6′4″ and 230 pounds, Calvin exploded when he hit the line and was fast enough to break loose for long runs. He was Rookie of the Year and made the Pro Bowl four times.

As a rookie, Calvin was so big and had so much talent that he spent his first two weeks in camp working at three positions— tight end, linebacker, and running back. But when he returned from playing in the College All-Star Game in Chicago, Tom Landry decided to leave him at running back and let him go.

In 1972 he became the club's first 1,000-yard rusher and repeated that achievement the following year.

Calvin was extremely bright and was interested in the many facets of life. During his first season with the Cowboys, he took a couple of theology courses at SMU. He wore his yellow Yale blazer with pride, and I'm sure a lot of his intellectual thoughts reflected what he learned there. He talked about politics, education, science, government, art, literature, and religion. These issues usually weren't relevant to football, but they were relevant to life.

In 1975, after six seasons with the Cowboys, Calvin received a lucrative offer to play for Hawaii

> *He talked about politics, education, science, government, art, literature, and religion.*

in the World Football League—and he took it. Upon leaving Dallas, he ranked second only to Don Perkins in career yardage.

Calvin currently works for the Cowboys organization as a consultant and specializes in working with troubled players.

His son is NBA player Grant Hill.

Roger Staubach

Roger reported to the Cowboys in '69 right after Don Meredith retired and Craig Morton became the starting quarterback—but everyone knew, including Coach Landry, that Roger never would be satisfied with being a backup.

As a junior out of Annapolis, Roger won the Heisman Trophy and the Maxwell Award in 1963 while leading the Midshipmen to a 9–2 record and a final No. 2 ranking in the nation.

He was a 10th-round draft pick in the 1964 NFL draft by the Dallas Cowboys, but due to his military commitment, he did not begin playing until 1969 as a 27-year-old rookie.

After graduating from the Naval Academy, Roger could have requested an assignment in the States, but he chose to volunteer for a one-year tour of duty in Vietnam, where he served as a supply officer for the United States Navy until 1967. He spent the rest of his naval career in the United States, serving out his military commission and playing football on various Naval service teams to prepare for his future career in the NFL.

In 1969 Roger resigned his commission just in time to join the Cowboys' training camp.

In 1971 Craig Morton began the season as the starter, but after a loss to the perennial doormat New Orleans Saints, Roger assumed the role.

However, in a game against the Chicago Bears in the seventh week of that season, Coach Landry alternated Staubach and

Morton on each play, sending in the quarterbacks with the play call from the sideline.

Dallas gained almost 500 yards of offense but suffered a 23–19 loss to a mediocre Bears squad that dropped the Cowboys to 4–3 for the season, two games behind the Washington Redskins in the NFC East race.

Roger assumed the full-time quarterbacking duties in a Week 8 victory over the St. Louis Cardinals and led the Cowboys to 10 consecutive victories, including their first Super Bowl victory, 24–3 over the Miami Dolphins.

Roger was named Most Valuable Player of Super Bowl VI on January 16, 1972, completing 12 out of 19 passes for 119 yards and two touchdowns, and rushing for 18 yards.

> *Roger could have requested an assignment in the States, but he chose to volunteer for a one-year tour of duty in Vietnam*

In 1972 he missed most of the season with a separated shoulder, but he relieved Morton in a divisional playoff against the San Francisco 49ers and threw two touchdown passes in the last 90 seconds to win the game 30–28. With that performance, he won back his regular job and did not relinquish it again during his career.

Nicknamed "Roger the Dodger" and "Captain Comeback" by his teammates and the media, he was All-NFC five times and played in six Pro Bowl games.

Roger retired from the Cowboys in 1979 and was inducted into the Ring of Honor in 1983 and into the Pro Football Hall of Fame in 1985.

STAUBACH'S STORIES

When Roger arrived at training camp, he was eager to become one of the boys. One day he and Dave Edwards decided that they were going to try snuff. Of course, Walt Garrison always carried at least 20 rolls of snuff with him at all times and offered some to Roger and Dave. This was just before we went into our team meeting.

Walt showed them what to do. He told them, "You get a big pinch and put it between your gum and your cheek." I noticed that Roger was reading the label on the Copenhagen tin, while Walt was giving them directions on how to use it. The tin read, "America's fine chewing tobacco."

We all put a pinch of the tobacco in our mouths and proceeded to the meeting.

After a while, I noticed that Roger was *chewing* the snuff instead of letting it sit between his gum and cheek. Snuff is finely ground, and when it is chewed it ends up going down your throat instead of allowing you to spit it out.

About 45 minutes later, the entire team witnessed both Dave and Roger running down the hall. Dave was throwing up as he was running, but Roger was able to make it to the bathroom in time. That was the last time Roger and Dave ever used snuff. Crazy things like that were what made training camp bearable.

Roger was the epitome of what Coach thought a quarterback should be, but even Captain America himself couldn't resist poking a little fun at Coach Landry.

One time in practice Roger and Coach Landry were working on a new goal-line play—a fake into the line and quarterback bootleg to the right.

Coach wasn't happy with the way Roger was executing the play, so he decided to show him how it was done. Tom had a problem with his knee, so he got behind the center, took the snap, made a really long fake to the back into the line, and then kind of limped to the right.

Coach told Roger to do the same thing as he had done with one exception—make the fake longer. So Roger took the snap, made the fake, and started running with a gimpy leg. Coach laughed at that one, and Roger learned that if he wanted to joke with Coach, timing was everything.

Mike Ditka

Mike Ditka was an All-American tight end out of the University of Pittsburgh who was drafted by Chicago in 1961. He was traded to the Eagles in 1967, and at the request of Coach Landry he was traded to the Cowboys in 1969. Mike was tough and rowdy, but Coach felt he had a few good years still left in him.

Our safeties, Charlie Waters and Cliff Harris, were all over Mike during practice. They used to taunt him about his moves. You don't taunt Mike Ditka.

One day Mike had had enough of Charlie and Cliff. While running one of his routes, Mike made his cut and forearmed both of them in the mouth. The taunting ceased.

While running one of his routes, Mike made his cut and forearmed both of them in the mouth.

Upon his retirement in 1972, Coach immediately hired Mike as an assistant coach. During his nine-year tenure the Cowboys made the playoffs eight times and won six division titles and three NFC championships.

Mike went on to successfully coach the Chicago Bears and won Super Bowl XX in 1986. In 1988 Ditka was inducted into the Pro Football Hall of Fame and for the past decade has been a strong advocate for the NFL's retired players.

His Gridiron Greats Assistance Fund is a nonprofit organization that provides financial assistance and coordination of social services to retired NFL players in dire need. It focuses on post-football-related issues, providing hands-on assistance to help retired players deal with hardships they may face after football.

DITKA'S STORIES

Mike Ditka joined the Cowboys in 1969 and was one of the toughest players I have ever known. If Coach had asked him to run through a brick wall, he probably would have.

One evening Mike walked into a restaurant and approached a table that had a stack of chairs sitting on top of it. Instead of taking the chairs down one by one, he knocked them down with his forearm and they came crashing down around him. He then called the rest of us over to sit down with him.

Without saying a word, we all did as he said. He had an impetuous temper and would blow up for the slightest reason. When he and Dan Reeves played golf together it could get ugly. They played golf like they played racquetball—getting mad, cussing, and throwing their racquets and golf clubs, often breaking them.

Class of 1970

Margene Adkins
Margene Adkins came to the Cowboys after being drafted in the second round of the 1970 NFL draft. As a teenager he joined the Ottawa Rough Riders of the CFL, was voted to the league's All-Star team in 1969 and was part of the 1969 championship Grey Cup team.

He joined the Cowboys as a wide receiver, but with high-caliber receivers such as Lance Alworth and Bob Hayes, the Cowboys decided to utilize Adkins primarily as a punt and kick returner. Although he was with us for only two seasons, he was a part of our 1971 Super Bowl VI championship team.

Duane Thomas

Duane was drafted by the Cowboys out of West Texas State in the first round of the 1970 NFL draft. In his rookie year he finished eighth in the NFL in rushing and led the league with 11 touchdowns in 1971.

Duane was a constant thorn in the side of Coach Landry. Coach would spend countless hours trying to talk to him, but the conversations were always one-sided—with Coach doing all the talking.

During a contract dispute with Cowboys management, Duane was traded before the 1971 season to the New England Patriots. He immediately got into an argument with Patriots coach John Mazur. Within a few days, the NFL granted the Patriots' request to void the trade, sending him back to the Cowboys.

Duane made it a point not to speak with any of the Cowboys players, coaches, or management for the entire season. At mealtime, he would eat alone in his room.

Despite his lack of communication, Duane successfully helped the Cowboys to their first Super Bowl win. Finally, at the end of the 1971 season, the Cowboys successfully traded Thomas to the San Diego Chargers.

Duane had all the talent in the world, but his attitude and demeanor overshadowed his tremendous skill and athleticism.

THOMAS'S STORIES

Duane played for Dallas for only two years, but his attitude and demeanor were known throughout the Cowboys organization. Although he was a great running back, he was also a pain in the butt, especially for Coach Landry. During the conversations he had with Duane when they didn't see eye-to-eye on various situations, Duane refused to speak.

In Duane's rookie year, he was an outstanding talent, got along with everyone, and worked hard at making the team. The following year he refused to talk to the players, the administration, and most of all, the media. He always seemed to be in an angry mood. During roll call, Duane refused to answer when his name was called. When Coach asked him why he wouldn't answer, Duane responded with, "You can see me. I'm sitting right here."

Once Duane hurt his knee during a game, and Jethro Pugh went over to see how he was. Thomas rudely answered, "Why you wanna know? You a doctor?"

During practice he would go off by himself, refusing to run drills with the defense. He would stand on the sideline chewing gum, and Coach didn't say a word to him.

Tom always had one set of standards and never veered off of them until Duane came along. I know Coach meant well, trying to help him, but it was a losing battle. Finally, Tom had had enough and traded Duane. Although he was one of the greatest backs in pro football, he bounced from team to team and eventually was gone from the NFL for good.

Cliff Harris and Charlie Waters

When you talk about one, you can't help but talk about the other. Cliff Harris and Charlie Waters were teammates on and off the field. Known as "the Twins," the safety tandems were the leaders of the secondary unit and became one of the most feared in the NFL.

Charlie was drafted by Dallas in 1970 out of Clemson University. Cliff's path to Dallas was a little different. He played for Ouachita Baptist College but was not chosen for the draft. Cliff played semipro ball for a few years, and in 1970 the Cowboys signed him as a free agent. With an invitation to training camp, Cliff met up with his future tandem partner.

They were so good together that they had a major effect on how the Cowboys selected their players on draft day. Dallas would go after skilled athletes and turn them into great linemen and linebackers. Their only concern would be stopping the run and getting to the quarterback while Cliff and Charlie would take care of pass coverage. Cliff was nicknamed "Captain Crash" by his teammates for his hard-hitting and fearless pursuit of ball carriers.

Cliff retired in 1979, and Charlie followed two years later. Charlie went on to be the defensive coordinator for the Denver Broncos and later for the Oregon Ducks.

In 1996 their partnership resumed when Cliff asked Charlie to join his sales staff and work for the Energy Transfer Group—an electricity supply company where Cliff is a partner.

In 2004 I had the honor of inducting Cliff into the Cowboys' Ring of Honor.

HARRIS'S STORY

Golden Richards was a wide receiver with lightning speed. He grew up in Utah, where he attended the University of Utah, but he completed his college career at the University of Hawaii. His nickname was "the Blond Flash" because of his quickness and his long blond hair.

Cliff Harris (also known as "Captain Crash") made an impression on every receiver he played against and with. He used to help the rookies out by jolting them in practice to keep them on their toes and letting them know that slacking during practice was completely unacceptable.

One day at practice Cliff noticed that Golden was running an inside route at half speed—not really trying. Cliff took it upon himself to let Golden know that he needed to pick up the pace. As Roger's pass hit his hands, Cliff hit him and knocked him out.

The following day Golden snuck a gift into Cliff's locker. It was a bright-yellow helmet with a siren and flashing red light on top. Golden told Cliff that he wanted him to wear it so he would know where he was at all times. Cliff laughed and told him that as long as he gave a hundred percent in practice he would have nothing to worry about.

The following day the rest of the team dared Cliff to wear the hat in practice. He took us on. He put on the hat, turned on the red flashing light and siren, and began running warmup laps on the field. Cliff didn't see Coach until he turned the corner, and from the look on Cliff's face, you could tell that he was nervous.

Coach Landry stared at Cliff with an expression of total disgust. "The look" had once again turned in Cliff's direction.

WATERS'S STORIES

Charlie's first preseason game as a Cowboy was against the Packers. He was a quarterback in college and absolutely idolized Bart Starr, Green Bay's Hall of Fame quarterback.

With a third-and-nine situation, Starr dropped back and looked downfield for an open receiver. A few seconds into the play he raised the ball to throw but changed his mind and tucked it under his arm, electing to scramble for the first down.

Bart crossed the line of scrimmage and began to veer toward the sideline as Charlie closed in on the veteran quarterback.

Waters and Starr collided, and the play ended two yards short of the first-down marker. Starr looked at Charlie and said, "Nice hit!"

Charlie was so excited that he replied in a childlike manner, "Could I have your autograph?"

Bart laughed and replied with, "Maybe after the game."

Another funny story about Charlie had to do with Gil Brandt, the Cowboys' vice president of personnel development. The Dallas players had a saying about Gil: "Gil Brandt knew we loved the game so much that we would play for nothing, so that's what he paid us…nothing."

When Gil Brandt showed up at Charlie's frat house on the Clemson campus to discuss his Cowboys contract, he was dressed in an Armani suit and a pair of alligator shoes. Charlie, being as young and naive as he was, was completely impressed by Brandt's attire and complimented him on his style of dress…especially his shoes.

Even though they didn't come to a contractual agreement at that time, Gil sent Charlie an identical pair of alligator shoes. Charlie was totally overwhelmed with the gesture.

They finally settled on a contract and Gil offered Charlie an additional $3,000 signing bonus to his $12,000 contract. With his bonus check, Gil enclosed an invoice for the alligator shoes and deducted the cost from Charlie's check!

Pat Toomay

Pat was drafted by the Cowboys in 1970 out of Vanderbilt. He had an enormous amount of talent and spent five seasons with Dallas.

Pat would have benefitted even more if the Cowboys had incorporated an intensive weight program at that time. Weighing around 240–250 pounds, he was a little light for the line. He played beside me, replacing George Andrie, who had retired.

It was my job to teach Pat to play the defensive line. He had great ability in rushing the passer. His height and speed contributed to that.

Pat, along with Larry Cole and Blaine Nye, was a member of the Zero Club. You could become a member of this club only if you received zero publicity from the press. Nevertheless, all were good football players, well educated, and quite intelligent. Anything they had to say was over our heads anyway.

Pat left Dallas the same year I retired, going on to play with Buffalo, Tampa Bay, and Oakland. He grew to become a very impressive defensive end.

Class of 1971

Billy Truax

Billy Truax was a tight end out of LSU who played with the Los Angeles Rams from 1964 to 1970 before coming to Dallas. He played the last three years of his career with our team. During that time we appeared in two Super Bowls—losing in Super Bowl V and winning our first in Super Bowl VI.

Billy was a very bright and very charming person who always had a smile on his face. He was a hard worker and a team player with great hands. He ended up like most tight ends with knee problems that I'm sure cut short his career.

We sure did appreciate all his help for the years he played with us in Dallas.

Lance Alworth

I played against Lance when I was in college. He was an All-American at the University of Arkansas where he played the running back position.

He was drafted in the first round of the 1962 draft by the San Francisco 49ers but ended up signing with the San Diego Chargers of the AFL after a bidding war with San Francisco. The Chargers moved him to the wide receiver position.

In 1971 Lance was traded to the Dallas Cowboys for his final two seasons—retiring in 1972. He was a great football player and a terrific runner. He was a wonderful, caring person who never had a bad word to say about anybody. He was a major asset to the team and scored one of the touchdowns in our game against Miami in Super Bowl VI. He would later be known to say that the two receptions he made in Super Bowl VI (one on a second and long and the other for the touchdown) were the two most important catches of his career.

In 1978 he became the first San Diego Charger and the first player to have played in the AFL to be inducted into the Pro Football Hall of Fame.

Toni Fritsch

When the NFL's conventional style of straight-on kicking was replaced by soccer-style kicking, Cowboys vice president of personnel development Gil Brandt took off for Europe to search for the best soccer-style kicker. Brandt found him in the form of a 5′7″, slightly balding, Austrian ex-superstar by the name of Toni Fritsch. Toni was past his prime for playing soccer, but not for kicking field goals and PATs.

When Toni first came to the Cowboys from Austria he didn't know anyone and didn't speak a word of English. We all felt pretty bad for him. His favorite thing to do was to watch cartoons in English.

One day at practice, Toni got his interpreter to bet Walt Garrison that he could make 12 consecutive field goals beginning at 20 yards and ending at 48 yards plus successfully landing the ball on the goal post each time. Walt took the bet, figuring it was easy money.

Toni successfully made each of the 12 field goals and successfully landed the ball on the goal post each time. Toni happily collected the $100 from Walt.

That night, Walt got Toni back. At the 11:00 curfew, Walt talked Toni into sneaking out of the dorm and driving into town to pick up a pizza for the guys. It wasn't very hard because Toni loved pizza and Walt was picking up the tab. Besides, Walt told Toni that kickers didn't have a curfew since all they did was kick the ball. Of course Toni believed him.

Tony made it out of the dorm without getting caught and picked up the pizza. While driving back to the facility a little too fast, the Thousand Oaks Police Department pulled him over.

Poor Toni. He neither had a license nor could speak English. As he pointed to his T-shirt, he tried to tell the officers, "Me Dallas Cowboy."

The officer responded with, "Sure you are, buddy, and I'm the Lone Ranger. You're going to jail!"

Gil Brandt had some connections and was able to get Toni released.

Toni may have successfully won the $100 bet, but Walt successfully got even with the con.

Everyone on the team liked Toni, and he was well respected by all. He was a great asset to the Cowboys organization.

In 2005 Toni collapsed at a restaurant in Vienna and died of heart failure at the age of 60.

Class of 1972

Robert Newhouse

Robert Newhouse came to the Cowboys out of Houston University. I actually got to see him play in college and immediately saw that he was a tough, aggressive player.

The first time I actually saw Robert he was in his street clothes. He appeared a little too small to be a fullback, but once I saw him in uniform I could see the massive size of his thighs, which, at that time, measured 38″. Then I watched him run and saw how well he could cut to gain yardage.

Robert received an engineering degree from Houston. That helped him a great deal in understanding Coach Landry's intricate system.

One day during practice, I decided to see just what Robert was made of. I ran straight at him to see how he would react. The hit he put on me was so devastating that it caused me to turn a complete flip!

> *The hit he put on me was so devastating that it caused me to turn a complete flip!*

Coach Landry saw what happened and immediately stopped practice. He said, "I wish I could show you all that play again because that is how I want my players to block. Newhouse is going to be all right."

He sure did put a hit on me, and from then on I didn't try to run through him. Sometimes I would jump over him, but I never again tried to run through him. He ended up becoming a great player and having a great career with Dallas.

Class of 1973

Billy Joe Dupree

Billy Joe came to the Cowboys near the end of my career. He was drafted in the first round out of Michigan State University. He was known as a great blocker and pass receiver and was one of the best tight ends of his era.

Our relationship began when he came to the Cowboys. Billy Joe not only was a superb tight end but also played extremely well on special teams.

After my retirement in 1974, Billy Joe was selected to three consecutive Pro Bowls and contributed to the 27–10 victory over the Denver Broncos in Super Bowl XIII. He played 11 years for the Cowboys and retired in 1983.

Today Billy Joe is involved with many charity works and is also a physical education teacher in Virginia. I have always had a great deal of respect and love for him. He is truly a fine person.

Golden Richards

John "Golden" Richards came to the Cowboys from Hawaii via Brigham Young University. As a wide receiver, Golden was well known for his incredible speed and also for his punt-returning skills.

He played five years for the Cowboys and was known for his long, golden blond hair that stuck out from under his helmet. The girls sure liked it! He was one of the first of many of what I called "the longhairs."

Golden was a tough player who could easily get open to catch the ball. In the Cowboys' Super Bowl XII win over the Broncos, he caught a TD pass from running back Robert Newhouse.

Harvey Martin

Harvey was drafted in the third round by the Cowboys out of East Texas State University. Nicknamed "Too Mean" by his team, he led the Cowboys in sacks for seven seasons.

Harvey was always special to me because we played side by side throughout his rookie season. I remember meeting him in training camp. He was a big, stout guy with a huge smile that would light up the room.

He was a big, stout guy with a huge smile that would light up the room.

"Coaching" Harvey on the line was probably one of my best jobs. I helped him by giving him signals as to whether the play would be a run or a pass. When I would say the word "Harvey" he always knew that the play would be run in our direction—in other words, don't go after the quarterback. I also taught him the flex defense, but when it came to pass rushing, Harvey didn't need any help.

When I retired and Randy White took my place at tackle, he and Harvey would wreak havoc on the opposing team's quarterback.

Harvey was a tremendous athlete who played in four Pro Bowls and was co-MVP in Super Bowl XII—an honor he shared with teammate Randy White. He played 11 seasons with the Cowboys, retiring in 1984.

Tex Schramm called him "one of the first great pass rushers of the Dallas organization."

Harvey passed away of pancreatic cancer in 2001. I consider myself fortunate to have had the chance to visit with him a month before his passing.

Class of 1974

Clint Longley

Clint played quarterback for Abilene Christian University and was drafted by the Cincinnati Bengals in the first round of the supplemental draft. He was immediately traded to Dallas.

Clint was really a character. He loved snakes and guns. He had two rattlesnakes as pets and used to bring them with him to training camp. Understandably, many members of the team stayed clear of Clint's room.

During Clint's rookie season he played extensively in only one game, but what a memorable game it was! We were playing the Redskins at Texas Stadium on Thanksgiving Day. Before the game began, the over-the-hill gang of Washington declared that they were going to take Roger out of the game.

In the third quarter and with a 13-point lead, the Redskins' prediction came true.

Enter Clint Longley. He may not have been a familiar name to Washington before the start of the game, but Clint made sure they remembered him by the end of the game.

In the third quarter he connected with Billy Joe Dupree for a touchdown, and in the fourth quarter with 45 seconds left in the game he threw another long pass to Drew Pearson to beat the Redskins. Needless to say, Clint "the Mad Bomber" Longley was the hero of the game.

But the accolades were short-lived. During Clint's second year with Dallas he believed that he would get a lot of playing time due to his performance in defeating the Redskins the year before. That was not the case, and Clint was on the bench most of the year—something that he resented deeply.

One morning during training camp the following season, Clint bad-mouthed Drew Pearson for incorrectly running a route. Roger Staubach overheard the remark and immediately corrected Clint. Clint reacted with a strong comment back to Roger, and an argument developed. Staubach remained calm and suggested that they resolve the disagreement after practice.

The argument was known only to Roger and Clint, so when the fight broke out between the two quarterbacks shortly after practice, everyone was stunned.

The two of them were duking it out on the baseball field among a cloud of dust. The fight was broken up, and it looked like Clint had taken the brunt of it.

Coach Landry brought the team together and said, "All ill feelings need to be left on the field and not carried forward. It's over!" But it wasn't quite yet.

During lunch, Charlie Waters decided to sit with Clint and hear his side of the story. Clint told Charlie that he knew how he could get traded. Knowing that he wouldn't get much playing time with Roger at the helm, Clint had asked Coach Landry to trade him in the off-season, but his request had been denied.

When Charlie asked how, Clint replied with, "You'll see." He got up and left the table.

We were all in the locker room getting dressed for the second practice of the day. Roger was putting on his shoulder pads when Clint popped him with a right cross.

Roger's head flew back and hit the wall behind him. He slumped to the floor.

Randy White held on to Clint, and we helped Roger up off the floor. As Roger became more aware of what had happened, his anger rose. He was trying to get to Clint but was being held back for his own good. Once the trainers took Roger out of the room, Randy released Clint.

Clint packed his bags and took the next flight home to Dallas. The following day Coach had him traded to the San Diego Chargers.

Ed Jones

Ed played defensive end with the Cowboys for 15 years and sacked opposing quarterbacks 106 times. He was nicknamed "Too Tall" by his teammates because of his 6′9″ height.

Coming from Tennessee State University, Ed was the number one draft choice of the Cowboys in 1974. I had the opportunity (as with Harvey Martin) to acclimate him to the Cowboys' Doomsday Defense.

In 1978 Ed decided that he would try professional boxing. He actually did quite well, as he won all of his bouts. In 1979 he returned to the Cowboys and remained with them until 1989.

Ed was selected All-Pro twice and played in 20 playoff games, including six NFC Championship Games and three Super Bowls. In his 15-year career with Dallas, Ed started in 203 games!

21

The Coaching Staff

Ermal Allen

When Ermal Allen joined the staff as offensive backfield coach in 1962, he was very intense and sometimes pretty outspoken. But through the years he mellowed out without losing any of his knowledge of football.

Ermal, who coached under Bear Bryant at Kentucky, was intelligent, was an excellent teacher, and had the gift of "instant recall"—he never forgot a thing.

When Tom Landry decided he needed an assistant who could handle the film and computer staff, Ermal was the ideal choice to serve in an advisory capacity for the Cowboys. Coach Landry referred to him and another Dallas coach, Neil Armstrong, as part of the Cowboys' "brain trust."

Raymond Berry

Raymond Berry, who coached our pass receivers in 1968 and '69, was another assistant coach headed for the Pro Football Hall of Fame. Raymond had just retired as a record-breaking receiver for the Baltimore Colts and came home to Texas to start his coaching career with the Cowboys.

He was very precise. As a player, he knew exactly how far it was to the sideline after he made his cut and looked for the ball.

On his very first day at training camp (in Dallas) he said that our practice field was too narrow. We measured it and found it to be short by five feet!

I guess all those years of running pass patterns and catching passes from a perfectionist like Johnny Unitas made him the phenomenal player that he was.

Raymond made it even tougher for us when he asked Coach Landry why Friday wasn't a regular workout day. He told Coach that the Colts always had a full workout day on Friday. Immediately Coach Landry transformed Friday from a light-workout day—without pads—to a full-workout day—with pads. We griped about it in the beginning, but in the long run we knew it was worth it.

In 1984 Coach Berry took over as the head coach of the New England Patriots. In 1985 the Pats went on to become the first team in NFL history to advance to the Super Bowl (XX) by winning three playoff games on the road.

That alone describes the impact Coach Berry had on us. Soon after he left, Dallas played in two Super Bowls. I guess you can't argue with success.

Jack Eskridge, Equipment Manager

Jack displayed favoritism toward the veterans of the team but showed a serious discontentment toward rookies.

In his first year as a Cowboy, Cliff Harris went to see Jack in the equipment cage to exchange a pair of socks that had holes in the heels.

If Jack had had it his way, they would have no say in anything.

Jack looked at the socks and said, "You can wear the ones with holes, rookie! I am just like the press and you can't get back to me!" Then he threw the socks back at Cliff.

Jack was also the guy who assigned a rookie his jersey number. Rookies had no say in the number they wore. If Jack had had it his way, they would have no say in anything.

Forrest Gregg

Another outstanding coach and fellow Hall of Fame member was Forrest Gregg.

In 1971 Forrest came (as a player) to the Cowboys from Green Bay. At the conclusion of the '71 season, he became part of Coach Landry's staff.

I used to talk to Forrest because he was such a competitive player and had so much experience. He always talked about how great it was to play under the Packers' head coach, Vince Lombardi.

He said that Coach Landry and Coach Lombardi were men of great character and distinction. His reason for playing his final year with Dallas was because he wanted to learn football from another great coach.

By playing for both Lombardi and Landry he had the opportunity to learn two completely different styles of football philosophy. Both philosophies would provide him deeper insights into football and prepare him for his future position as an NFL head coach.

Forrest was a part of six championships, five of them with the Green Bay Packers, before closing out his tenure with the Dallas Cowboys with a win in Super Bowl VI.

He went on to serve as head coach of three teams: the Cleveland Browns, the Cincinnati Bengals, and the Green Bay Packers.

Jim Myers

Jim Myers was on Coach Landry's staff longer than anyone else. First, he was the offensive line coach and later, the assistant head coach.

He arrived in Dallas in early 1962 shortly after he left his head coaching position at Texas A&M. He remained with the Cowboys until 1986.

Jim was a former marine and did everything by the book. His coaching technique was fair and consistent, tough and smart. He was respected by all of us.

As the Cowboys began to recruit more and more talented players, our offensive line became one of the best in pro football, and Coach Myers is credited with that.

Dick Nolan

The first time I ever saw Dick Nolan he was blowing smoke rings on a huge billboard in Times Square in New York City.

The advertisement was for Camel cigarettes. Back in those days everyone smoked, and it was legal for an athlete to represent the tobacco and liquor industry for payment. From 1954–1957 and 1959–1962, Dick Nolan played defensive back for the New York Giants. With New York at the hub of the advertising business world, players from the Giants were often asked to appear in commercials.

He also played for the Chicago Cardinals and later, the Dallas Cowboys. He retired from the Cowboys after the '62 season.

Dick and Tom had ties from their Giants days together, so Nolan fit right in when he became the Cowboys' defensive secondary coach (1963–1968).

As a coach he quickly developed a good rapport and reputation with the team. He later became the first man from Coach Landry's staff to become a head coach—moving to San Francisco in 1968 through 1975 and building three playoff teams with the 49ers (1970–1972), twice missing the Super Bowl by only one game (1970–1971).

From 1978 to 1980, Dick was the head coach for the New Orleans Saints. He was the first Saints head coach to win eight games in a single season (1979) and finish the season 8–8. But in 1980, after an 0–12 start, Dick was released by the Saints.

As a side note: exactly 37 years to the day, his son Mike signed on with the 49ers as head coach.

With his head coaching career behind him, Dick once again returned to the Cowboys staff. I know Coach Landry was glad to have him back.

Ray Renfro

Another fellow Texan, Ray Renfro joined the Cowboys organization in 1968. Ray had an outstanding 12-year career (1952–1963) as a wide receiver with the Cleveland Browns.

His job was to be in charge of the passing game and to teach the players through his experience and expertise. He spent five years with the Dallas organization. I'm sure he made a positive impact on the Cowboys.

Incidentally, his son Mike Renfro also played his last few years with the Cowboys and did a great job.

Gene Stallings

Gene Stallings was a man of high character and principles. I always thought he was as fine a man as Coach Landry.

Coach Stallings was involved in football his whole life. He played under Coach Bear Bryant at Texas A&M, and in 1958 Gene accepted an assistant coaching position and joined Coach Bryant's coaching staff at Alabama.

At age 29, Gene became the head coach of Texas A&M, where he remained for seven seasons and won the Southwest Conference in 1967.

He did a fine job and was a good influence on our team.

Coach Stallings joined the Cowboys as a defensive secondary coach in 1972 and remained with the team for 14 years as an assistant coach. He did a fine job and was a good influence on our team.

In 1986 he became the head coach for the St. Louis Cardinals and in 1990 returned to the University of Alabama as head coach.

Coach Stallings finished the 1991 season with an 11–1 record and beat the University of Colorado in the 1991 Blockbuster Bowl.

COACH STALLINGS'S STORY

After our loss in Super Bowl V, Coach Landry wanted to make some attitude adjustments within the secondary defensive unit, so he hired Gene Stallings to replace Bobby Franklin.

Although Gene was unaware of it, he was about to take on the challenge of a lifetime. At practice you could tell that he was a no-nonsense guy. He told the team that he was here because, "I got my ass fired as the head coach of Texas A&M. I won the national championship one year, and the next year they fired me! So I am not in a good mood!"

The rookies thought they were really in for it, but the veterans—Mel Renfro, Cornell Green, and Herb Adderley—just looked at each other with doubt.

Next, Coach Stallings said, "Now we're gonna do some hittin'!" That's where the vets drew the line. Mel slowly walked over to Gene and in a soft voice said, "Gene, we don't hit." Gene replied with, "Well, we'll see about that."

The rookies busted their butts running through the tackle drills while the uniforms of Mel, Cornell, and Herb remained clean and untouched. Following the lead of the vets, the rookies decided to do the same. Coach Stallings was beginning to learn about the system.

But as time went on, we all learned—including the vets—what an excellent coach and teacher Gene really was. He really did know football, and in time we adjusted to the fact that it was his way or no way.

Ernie Stautner

Defensive lineman Ernie Stautner was drafted by the Pittsburgh Steelers in 1950 and remained with the team until 1963. He was selected to nine Pro Bowls throughout his 14-year career.

He was an assistant coach with the Cowboys from 1965 to 1988, served as the team's defensive coordinator from 1973 to 1988, and scouted for the team from 1988 to 1989.

Ernie was one of the toughest coaches I ever had the pleasure of working with. This Hall of Fame defensive lineman filled a tremendous void for the Cowboys when Tom Landry hired him as our defensive line coach. Ernie had coached a couple of years for the Washington Redskins prior to coming to the Cowboys.

Coach Stautner later became the defensive coordinator, along with Jerry Tubbs.

We hadn't had a defensive line coach for two years. Because we didn't have anyone to push us, the defensive linemen were somewhat lackadaisical when it came to running wind sprints and working out after practice. Ernie changed all that. He worked our tails off!

He helped me a lot with some of my defensive moves, and he taught me how to head-butt.

He was a great guy and he gave us the benefit of his experience. He helped me a lot with some of my defensive moves, and he taught me how to head-butt.

If an opponent tried to hold me, I would charge into him with my head. If that player lowered his head, we'd butt heads. While my opponent had his head down, I would grab his jersey and get around him. It worked just like Ernie said it would.

COACH STAUTNER'S STORY

When Ernie Stautner played for Pittsburgh, his roommate was none other than the great Bobby Layne. As a matter of fact, Ernie was Bobby's bodyguard.

One night Bobby took Buddy Dial and a player who was picked up by the Steelers from the 49ers by the name of Dickie Moegle to dinner.

After a night of bar hopping, they all ended up at the Hurricane Bar in the Hill District of Pittsburgh.

Bobby, who was totally inebriated, took a seat at the bar next to Ernie, who was also three sheets to the wind. Bobby was telling both Buddy and Dickie how tough Ernie was. He told them, "Ernie Stautner is the toughest SOB that ever lived and I'll prove it!"

Just then, Layne took a long drag off his cigarette and turned his barstool toward Ernie. Ernie stuck out his tongue and Bobby put his cigarette out on Ernie's tongue. Stautner let out a boisterous laugh, turned his barstool back toward the bar, and pounded down his drink.

"See," said Bobby. "The toughest SOB who ever lived!"

Fourth Quarter
Life after Football

22

Battle Scars

WHEN YOU ARE A PROFESSIONAL FOOTBALL PLAYER, pain becomes a part of your life that you experience every day of your life for the rest of your life. Throughout the regular season your body is inflicted with such punishment that it hurts just to get out of bed in the morning. Knowing that you have a responsibility and obligation to your-

> *When you are a professional football player, pain becomes a part of your life*

self, the team, and the coach is the adrenaline rush needed to get you through the pain of the game on Sunday.

Some of the injuries that are experienced on the football field are minor and in time will heal themselves. But there are times when the injuries are severe and require surgery. This type of physical damage can and will cause debilitating, lifelong effects on the player.

Back in the early days of the sport, most guys played with the pain or they didn't get paid. How's that for an incentive? Old clichés such as, "Tough it out!" "Don't let the team down!" "Walk it off!" and "Know the difference between pain and injury!" were common. Also, these guys played both offense and defense and were getting paid an average of only $5,000–$6,000 a year.

Former 49ers offensive tackle and Hall of Famer Bob St. Clair, who had five teeth knocked out on a blocked punt, was sent to the sideline to have cotton stuffed in the orifices where his teeth once stood and then returned to the field in time for the next play.

Another time St. Clair broke his shoulder a few minutes into the first quarter. The trainer taped his shoulder in place, and he finished out the rest of the game. After the final gun sounded, Bob, along with 49ers defensive tackle and Hall of Fame member Leo Nomellini, *drove himself to the hospital!* Now that's desire and dedication to the game!

The NFL that I played in was a little more humane. But when it came to pain and injuries, the hurt was the same. Like my teammates, I had to learn to play with the pain—to eventually block it out so I could play with as little distraction as possible.

When a player was injured, the first method of treatment was usually the training room hot tub—or what we called it back then, "the whirlpool." Right next to the whirlpool was a 50-gallon tub that was filled with ice. Injured players would first soak the injured area in the hot tub for about 15 to 20 minutes and then surround the damaged extremity in the ice.

In order to have a player healed and back on the field in the shortest amount of time, the Cowboys were furnished with the most technologically up-to-date medical equipment. Besides the hot and cold tubs, we also had ultrasound, heat packs, an acupuncturist, a neck brace for compressed thoracic injuries, and many other modern medical resources.

If the first method of treatment was unsuccessful, then you would advance to the second level. Enter Dr. Marvin Knight.

As I mentioned earlier, Dr. Knight was the man who operated on my dad's leg.

He was definitely old school. His demeanor reflected that of a grumpy old man, but behind that rough exterior was a talented and brilliant doctor. He lived outside Dallas in a town called Muenster. Every week he would drive down to the Cowboys' facility to treat injured players. He also traveled with us on away games.

Like Coach Landry, Dr. Knight understood the difference between pain and injury. When examining a player who thought he had been injured but wasn't, Dr. Knight would say, "You're not injured. Get your ass back out there!"

Dr. Knight always had a cure for any type of football injury. If your recuperation was coming along too slowly, the doctor had a "fast way to get back in the game" cure—a cortisone shot with a touch of Novocain. It would numb the pain so you could go out and perform, but the long-range effects caused massive debilitation of the injured area(s).

My rookie year with the team was a real eye-opener for me. I had been fortunate enough to have played football throughout grade school, high school, and college without receiving any major injuries—or at least I thought I hadn't.

Upon completing my first physical with the Cowboys, I was informed that the X-rays showed that I had a cracked vertebra in my neck. It then occurred to me that while I was at TCU, I had experienced a terrible pain in my neck after getting hit hard in a game. Thank goodness it wasn't bad enough to cause any form of paralysis.

My rookie year was also the season that I acquired most of my injuries. In 1961 we had 33 players on the squad. The younger players were required to not only play on all of the

I was so naive that I didn't know to tape my wrists and fingers together before games.

kicking teams—kickoffs, kickoff returns, punt returns, and extra points—but also to play their regular positions on the field.

I was so naive that I didn't know to tape my wrists and fingers together before games. Early in the season, in either the second game against the Vikings or the third game against the Browns, I broke my right thumb. It turned out to be a compound fracture. The bone had penetrated the skin and was now exposed.

Dr. Knight took my thumb and gave it a few sharp pulls until the bone snapped back into place. He taped it in place right there on the field. It was later set with a cast and I played with it like that for the remainder of the season. The problem with the cast was that each time I made a play, the bone would break through the skin. At the end of each game the old cast would have to be removed and a new one put in its place. Dr. Knight's methods might have been a little unconventional, but they eventually did the job.

In the fourth game of my rookie season, we played against the Vikings in Minnesota. I was covering a kickoff. While running down the field, one of my players was blocked from behind, causing him to fall on me.

The blow was so hard that it knocked me high in the air, and I landed on my knee on top of the pitcher's mound. The fall caused my knee to hyperextend, thus tearing the medial collateral ligaments.

With this type of injury I was told I wouldn't be playing the following week, but on game day Coach Landry came into the locker room and told me that he didn't have any reserves who could take my place. I would have to play—torn ligaments and all.

Dr. Knight shot me up with Novocain and taped my knee, and I went out and played. My leg was so heavily taped that it was stiff. Obviously, I didn't have a great game.

During our team meeting on Monday we reviewed the film of our last game. Coach Landry—who was always very honest—said, "Bob, you didn't have a very good game!"

At that very moment I was thinking, "I wasn't even supposed to play, Coach!" But out of respect, I didn't say a word.

Anyway, I finished out the season playing with a broken thumb and torn medial collateral ligaments in my left knee. Fortunately, I was able to get my knee back in shape during the off-season and didn't require surgery. Back in the '60s, knee surgery could end a player's career.

I injured my leg a second time in 1964 during a scrimmage at training camp. I was on top of the pile when someone jumped on top of me and landed directly on my knee, and I sustained strained ligaments.

During a game against the Packers, one of their players accidentally kicked my hand and broke two of my fingers. The ligaments had been torn loose from the fingers and it was incredibly painful. As I approached the sideline, Dr. Knight was waiting.

He examined my hand, my fingers pointing in every direction but the right one. Again, Dr. Knight snapped them back into place, taped them up, and sent me back into the game.

For the next game and every game thereafter throughout my football career, I learned how to tape outside and in between my fingers (my hands giving the appearance of the webbed feet of a duck) so they wouldn't get broken or separated.

For the next game and every game thereafter throughout my football career, I learned how to tape outside and in between my fingers (my hands giving the appearance of the webbed feet of a duck) so they wouldn't get broken or separated.

Later in my career, I broke a bone in the lower part of my forearm and immediately learned how to tape my wrists before taking my stance on the field.

By my fifth year with the team, I began arriving to the stadium dressing room two hours before the game. Game preparation consisted of a soak in the whirlpool to loosen up the muscles and having the trainer tape my ankles, knees, fingers, and wrists.

Before playing the Steelers in Dallas, I had been suffering from a painful bone spur that was located on my right heel. Prior to the start of the game, Dr. Knight decided to inject my heel with cortisone. The pain from the needle entering the bone spur was so unbelievable that I almost passed out. Boy, did it hurt! I broke out in a sweat.

> *The pain from the needle entering the bone spur was so unbelievable that I almost passed out.*

Noticing my condition, Dr. Knight said, "Oh, I probably should have used a little Novocain with that shot." My immediate thought was, "If I ever need surgery, I definitely don't want you as my doctor!"

Once the numbness set in, I was ready to go out on the field. During one of the plays, I was able to get by their offensive guard and was on my way to tackle their quarterback, Terry Bradshaw. Just as I was ready to bring Terry down I was clipped from behind.

The hit knocked loose the bone spur that was situated on the heel of my right foot. At the moment of impact, the pain had subsided—for good. After the game, Dr. Knight told me that I had saved myself from having an operation.

In 1972 I injured my lower back while practicing out on the field. By the end of practice my back had tightened up so much that I decided to get into the whirlpool. I later discovered that it wasn't heat that I needed, but cold.

Within a few minutes the muscles of my back had tightened up so badly that three of my teammates had to help me out of the whirlpool. They helped me dress and drove me to the hospital.

I was immediately put in traction and was given muscle relaxers to loosen up my back and relieve the pain. I ended up missing two days of practice. The following Friday the team flew out to San Francisco to get ready to play the 49ers in a playoff game at Candlestick Park. The doctor and I flew out on Saturday to join the team. I was given about 50 shots of Novocain in my lower back, which made it possible for me to play the first quarter. The pain returned at the beginning of the second half, and I was out for the remainder of the game. Luckily we won, and I was able to play the following week.

I was given about 50 shots of Novocain in my lower back, which made it possible for me to play the first quarter.

In 1973 during a game with the Denver Broncos, I picked up a fumble and began running it in for a touchdown when a Denver player grabbed me by the face mask while two other Broncos held me by my legs. Cowboys safety Cliff Harris tried coming to my rescue but instead of hitting the Bronco players, he hit me. My legs split in opposite directions, and I ended up tearing my hamstring in two. Immediately my leg filled up with fluid and blood and the skin became discolored, causing a purple and red bruise to appear. It took quite a long time for me to rehabilitate the leg.

Other injuries included a right shoulder separation, a jammed thumb, dislocated fingers, and a hip pointer, which at first I thought was a broken hip due to the intense pain. In my 14th year, a neck injury ended my career and forced me to retire. I still have that pain to this day.

Back in the '60s and '70s we played with a lot of tape, a lot of Novocain, and a lot of guts.

Postcareer Illness

Although I sustained many injuries while playing with the Cowboys, the life-threatening illness that I contracted last year was worse than any gridiron injury I've ever experienced. And to think that it all began with a few broken teeth that were kicked out during my football career.

At TCU I had a few teeth knocked out on the field. I lost several more when I was playing pro ball. If you cracked a tooth back then, the dentist didn't try to save it. They just pulled it out and put in a bridge.

This past year I broke one of my dental bridges. After discussing my options with my dentist, I decided to have implants put in.

During the procedure, my sinuses became infected. I needed to take antibiotics for the infection, but in the process of taking the medicine, my digestive system became irritated. The pain was unbearable—especially when I ate. I ended up losing 20 pounds due to IBS (irritable bowel syndrome) and now have to be extremely careful about my diet.

As professional football players, we all played with injuries and pain, but we also played with ambition, desire, and determination.

By the way, my implant bill was $28,000, but for what it's worth, at least I can chew my food again.

In the game of professional football your body tells you when it's time to quit. Injuries don't heal as fast as they did in your younger years, and the Novocain injections become more and more frequent with every game. Even though the mind is willing, the body can no longer perform.

As professional football players, we all played with injuries and pain, but we also played with ambition, desire, and determination—and all for the love of the game.

Would I do it all over again? Would I suit up on Sunday and line up in those trenches for another 14 years?

You bet I would!

23

Postgridiron Employment

AFTER WINNING SUPER BOWL VI, we were all invited to a party at the Airport Hilton that was hosted by Cowboys owner Clint Murchison. Charlie Pride sang at the event, and it was just wonderful to share it all with my family and friends.

The following morning I got up especially early, as Roger Staubach, John Niland, Rayfield Wright, Mel Renfro, and I were getting ready to leave for the Pro Bowl game that was being played in Los Angeles.

I decided to take a walk outside to where the party was staged the night before. All that remained was a vacant parking lot and a lot of trash from the party. While waiting for the other guys to show, I started thinking about the fact that we were finally world champions, but at the same time I realized that winning the Super Bowl was the last goal that I had wanted to achieve. I had basically done it all.

> *I realized that winning the Super Bowl was the last goal that I had wanted to achieve. I had basically done it all.*

Just then I felt a hollowness, almost a depression, come over me. I knew that I loved the game and that I loved my teammates, but the desire to play that once ruled my heart was now no more than a memory.

I began searching for something more out of life—and that something was money. I decided to go into the beer distribution business; my career in the alcoholic-beverage industry had started long before my retirement from football.

In 1964 a Coors distributor invited me to his home in Odessa, Texas. He was a real character named Shotgun Henry.

When I arrived at the Midland-Odessa airport, I was greeted by Shotgun. We got into his car and drove to his home. It was absolutely gorgeous. There was a beautiful swimming pool out back, and the entire property was surrounded by an enormous fence.

We got to know each other and soon became good friends. Shotgun introduced me to some of the other Coors distributors from the West Texas and Fort Worth areas. They told me that it would be a good idea if I applied for a distributorship with Coors because they were going to expand their distribution in Texas.

I contacted my good friend and accountant Don Caylor and told him about the possibility of owning a beer distributorship. I asked him if he would be interested in partnering with me if and when a distributorship came to be. He agreed.

During the 1974 season, I was contacted by the Coors Brewery informing me of their expansion plans. They inquired as to whether or not I was still interested in applying for a distributorship. An application had been enclosed with the letter. Don and I filled out the application and in July of 1975 were awarded the Coors distributorship in Waco, Texas.

Neither Don nor I had any experience in the beer business.

We worked extremely hard to build the offices and warehouse, buy the trucks, and hire the staff. Neither Don nor I had any experience in the beer business, so we contacted a group of people who could help us. In November 1975, we were officially open for business.

About that same time I began to host the *Bob Lilly Radio Show* and was also the color commentator on radio station KRLD in Dallas.

In 1980 I signed with Black and Decker to do a series of commercials for their company. I made a total of 42 commercials in three states—New York, California, and Pennsylvania. In the meantime I had become friends with Mr. Decker, the son of the company's founder, and continued sponsoring Coors products for the next five years.

Financially, my beer distributorship was very good to me. I made a great deal of money—more than I ever made when playing for the Cowboys. I had the chance to meet a lot of nice people, but I never really felt comfortable with the business.

One day while driving home on Interstate 35, I noticed a pickup truck that had overturned on the freeway. I pulled over to see if I could help. When I opened the door of the overturned vehicle, beer cans spilled out, and there was a group of teenage boys in the truck. They had all been drinking beer.

When I opened the door of the overturned vehicle, beer cans spilled out.

I immediately felt that the Lord was punishing me for setting a poor example for these kids. With the help of my wife, Ann, our friends, and our church, I once again heard the Word of the Lord. I decided to sell my distributorship. I told Don that I had to make some changes in my life and the business was one of them. Thankfully he understood. God answered my prayers quickly. We had a buyer for the distributorship before I even finished praying!

24

The Ring of Honor and the Hall of Fame

THE DALLAS COWBOYS RING OF HONOR encircles the inside wall of Texas Stadium. The area is located above the main seating bowl and below the suite level.

Within that ring are the inscribed names of former players, their uniform numbers and years of service, as well as coaches and administrators and their years of service, who have made outstanding contributions to the Cowboys organization.

Upon my retirement in 1974, Tex Schramm's plan for memorializing the great players and administrative members of the organization was well under way.

It all began with the jerseys. The fans wanted Tex to retire the numbers of the Cowboys greats. This does not reflect, though, the era of the 1960s. Some of the fans from that period of time thought it would be appropriate if Tex could retire all the jerseys with all the Cowboys still in them.

The 1970s saw the Cowboys in the win column and establishing themselves as an NFL legacy. In 1971 the team finally made the move to the new Texas Stadium.

Traditionally, jerseys are retired in honor of the player who made that number outstanding. Once the player has officially retired, his number is never to be worn again by any other player. In Schramm's case, he didn't believe that a jersey should be retired because it would then just become another relic from the past. He wanted something that the fans could physically see every time they entered Texas Stadium—and that something was the Ring of Honor.

Just for the record, linebacker Chuck Howley, who was drafted in the first round by the Bears in 1958 before coming to the Cowboys, and linebacker Randy White, who was drafted in the first round in 1975, both wore No. 54. Both are in the Ring of Honor—each with No. 54 next to their names.

On the other hand, even though the Cowboys do not officially retire jerseys, my number, No. 74, and Roger Staubach's number, No. 12, have not been worn by any other Cowboys players.

In early November 1975 I received a call from the team's administrative office notifying me that I was going to be honored at Bob Lilly Day at Texas Stadium. In a game against the Philadelphia Eagles on November 23, 1975, I suited up in ole No. 74 for the very last time. At halftime I became the first recipient of the Ring of Honor. I was then escorted into a beautiful convertible and driven around the field in front of thousands of cheering fans.

At halftime I became the first recipient of the Ring of Honor.

Upon completing the pass, I stepped out of the car and onto the middle of the field. Owner Clint Murchison Jr., Tex Schramm, Coach Landry, and the entire Cowboys team gathered around to honor me.

In attendance were people who had represented my entire Cowboys career. Chuck Howley was on hand to represent my old teammates. Lee Roy Jordan, Tex Schramm, Coach Landry, and owner Clint Murchison were there to represent the current organization. And Jerry Kramer, former lineman with the Green Bay Packers, was there to represent my opponents.

Not only was I showered with accolades, but the organization presented me with a brand-new Pontiac station wagon. The gifts didn't stop there. My teammates presented me with a beautiful Browning shotgun—which, by the way, was and still is a very expensive firearm. It remains one of my most prized, not to mention priceless, possessions. And last, but certainly not least, the current team doctor, Dr. Pat Evans (who had replaced Dr. Knight) presented me with a bird dog. To say I was overwhelmed would be an understatement.

The speeches made by former teammates, coaches, and administrative people were full of praise and respect, but none more so than the compliment I received from Coach Landry. He said, "In my lifetime, there hasn't been a player as good as Bob Lilly. And I don't expect to ever see another one. He is the greatest player I've ever coached." I was deeply touched by his words.

At the conclusion of the ceremony, Coach Landry once again took over the microphone and said, "And now for the finale."

I looked over and saw some of the players pulling on a cord that was connected to a cover located underneath the press box. The ropes had gotten tangled, and they were having trouble untangling them. Finally the team was able to pull off the cover, and there for all to see was my name in huge letters followed by the years I had played for the Cowboys. The crowd gave me a standing ovation. I had been the first recipient of what would become known as the Ring of Honor. This event proved to be one of the happiest days of my life. By the way, the Cowboys beat the Eagles that day, 27–17. That made the day an even better one.

There for all to see was my name in huge letters followed by the years I had played for the Cowboys.

When the game was over, we celebrated in a big way. So big that Tex and the rest of the Cowboys organization had decided to host an annual Reunion/Ring of Honor Weekend to share with current and former team members and coaches.

As the Ring of Honor's first inductee, I have the added distinction of returning to Texas Stadium to welcome each new member into the Ring. I truly believe that this continuity of fellowship, brotherhood, and friendship has kept the players close to this day.

Since the time my name appeared in the Ring of Honor (1975), only nine other players received this recognition through the first three decades of its existence (between 1976 and 1994), therefore making this award of athleticism and character a coveted accolade to the vision of its creator, general manager Tex Schramm.

The nine other Ring of Honor recipients in the first 30 years were Don Meredith (1976), Don Perkins (1976), Chuck Howley (1977), Mel Renfro (1981), Roger Staubach (1983), Lee Roy Jordan (1989), Tom Landry (1993), Tony Dorsett (1994), and Randy White (1994).

Since 2001 I have also had the opportunity to present Bob Hayes (2001), Cliff Harris (2004), and Rayfield Wright (2004) with this exclusive award. Tex became only the 12th individual selected to the Ring of Honor, but sadly the award was given posthumously in October 2003—only three months after his passing.

On Monday, September 19, 2005, at Texas Stadium, the Dallas Cowboys played their formidable foes, the Washington Redskins. During that *Monday Night Football* halftime ceremony, an unprecedented three former Cowboys All-Stars were simultaneously inducted into the Ring of Honor. I had the privilege of presenting the award to quarterback Troy Aikman, wide receiver Michael Irvin, and running back Emmitt Smith.

There is one thing that I would like to change about the Ring of Honor—it's too restrictive. It was designed to be exclusive, but that's why they have the Pro Football Hall of Fame in Canton, Ohio. I think the Ring of Honor should be for those players who have performed consistently well over a long period of time. It should also be representative of each era. There should be a committee of representatives made up of those players who would be consulted as to who gets voted in. The owners and administrative team are not as familiar with the candidates as are the guys who literally played next to them; therefore, it would be logical for the players rather than the administration to vote for the recipient of the award.

The Hall of Fame

Being inducted and enshrined into the Pro Football Hall of Fame in Canton, Ohio, is the highest form of achievement that can be bestowed upon any professional football player. But becoming enshrined into the Hall was not one of my goals when I played for the Cowboys. I feel that this honor was a result of the accomplishments and goals that I set for myself along the way.

The Hall opened its doors on September 7, 1963, where at that time 17 charter inductees were enshrined into the annals of pro football history. This elite membership is home to 247 men. Within that distinguished group, 10 are from the Dallas Cowboys.

I never really thought much about being inducted into the Hall. I had always envisioned those great men as my heroes—a category that I never saw myself a part of.

In early January of 1980, I received a call from Pete Elliott of the Pro Football Hall of Fame informing me that I had been selected to the Hall's Class of 1980. A few weeks later, my wife,

I never really thought much about being inducted into the Hall.

Ann, and I were flown to Honolulu, Hawaii, for the Pro Bowl. The Hall's most recent class was going to be introduced at the game.

At halftime they presented me, along with three of my distinguished colleagues who had been my gridiron heroes when I was growing up. The first was cornerback Herb Adderley, a former Dallas teammate of mine (1970–1972) who went into the Hall as a Green Bay Packer. Next was defensive end David Deacon "Mr. Sack" Jones from the Los Angeles Rams, The last one was a center, Jim Otto ("00") from the Oakland Raiders. So there were four of us in my "class" of inductees to the Hall in 1980.

The honor was actually twofold for me personally, as I was the first Dallas Cowboy to receive this prominent recognition. It was at the Pro Bowl presentation that my going to Canton had finally sunk in. I can't tell you how thrilled I was.

We arrived in Canton in July of 1980 with approximately 50 of our family members and friends. Included in this group were my four children: Bob Jr., who was 18 years old; our daughters Michelle and Chris, who were 16 and 15; and our youngest, Mark, who was 5. I remember my son Bob Jr. being asked by reporters, "What's it like to be Bob Lilly's son?" Bobby answered, "Well, sir, it's all I've ever known." Cute answer, wasn't it?

From the time our plane landed at the tiny airport, the activities and events that had been set up for us by the Hall became nonstop. The pace was unbelievable.

That first night we attended the board of director's dinner. It was casual and gave me and my family a chance to meet and dine with the other enshrinees and members of the Hall.

The next morning the enshrinees and their presenters attended the Mayor's Breakfast. We met and ate with the mayor of Canton, the board of directors, Canton's Chamber of Commerce staff, and the Hall of Fame administrative staff.

After breakfast, we were given a tour of the Hall. It was the first time I had ever been there. Viewing the bronze busts of those "heroes of the hall" and reading the plaques of their gridiron accomplishments made me realize just how much football had meant to me and how it had changed my life.

Upon completion of the tour, we were off to the Enshrinees' Luncheon, which is now known as the Nitschke Luncheon—named after the great Green Bay Packers linebacker Ray Nitschke. The luncheon was held at the beautiful Brookside Country Club in Canton and is strictly a Hall of Fame "members only" event.

The new inductees were escorted into a room to listen to the testimonies of the past members. They talked about what the Hall has meant to them—that it is an elite fraternity of men and a team that you can never be cut from. They also stressed the importance of upholding and representing the image—never to embarrass the Hall by your actions. The following part of the program was saved for Ray Nitschke.

His gravelly voice bellowed with furious veracity as he gave his famous "fire and brimstone" speech. His words regarding correct protocol and behavior shook the walls of the building. One becomes extremely humbled upon leaving the Nitschke Luncheon.

That night the enshrinees were introduced at the civic dinner and received their pale yellow "members only" Hall of Fame jackets. Each enshrinee was individually congratulated by every Hall of Fame member in attendance. It was a night I will never forget.

The following morning we rode in the Timken Grand Parade. The parade route extends 2.2 miles and accommodates a crowd of over 200,000 spectators—not to mention the millions viewing the procession on the national television broadcast.

The parade featured well over a hundred entries, including spectacular floats, marching bands, returning Hall of Fame members, and the 1980 enshrinees and their presenters.

In between each event, we were swarmed by the media for television, radio, and press interviews. By the time the actual enshrinement took place on the steps of the Hall of Fame, we were completely exhausted.

At the ceremony each enshrinee and his presenter was instructed not to speak beyond the 10-minute time limit. Of course, not many people followed those instructions. With all the excitement, anxiety, and people that you had to remember to thank, you couldn't possibly say it all within the given time span. Nowadays, they have a little red light that blinks on and off to let you know that your speaking time is up. Still, not too many people pay attention to the blinking light.

His speech was as eloquent and refined as the man himself.

The choice of who my presenter would be was not a hard one to make. The person who immediately came to mind was Coach Landry. He had to take time off from training camp at Thousand Oaks, California, and fly all night just so he could perform in the ceremony the following day. It was such a wonderful thing for him to do for me. His speech was as eloquent and refined as the man himself. I was very honored to have Coach present me to the audience.

Everyone talked about breaking down and crying while giving a speech, but what I didn't know was that the Hall of Fame members pretty much took bets as to which enshrinee would be the first to break down and cry. Whether or not I was the first one, I ended up crying halfway through my enshrinement speech.

At the time of my induction, my mom had been ill and was hospitalized in Texas. As I addressed the audience, I spoke of the love, support, and encouragement that both my mother and father had shown me throughout the years. The only regret I had that day was that my dad, who had passed away in early 1970, and my former TCU coach Abe Martin were not alive to share in the joy and pleasure of that incredible day. It was at this time that my speech became focused on the men in my life who had encouraged me to play the game of football.

I spoke first about my dad, then continued on with my junior high and high school coaches. They were all great men, especially my Pendleton High School coach, Don Requa. From there I talked about Abe Martin and how I had come full circle with Hall of Fame member Sammy Baugh. And last, but definitely not least, I talked about Coach Landry and his staff with the Cowboys.

Being inducted into the Hall of Fame was beyond my wildest dreams. At the completion of my induction speech, I realized that I was now on that same elite team as the Sammy Baughs and the Jim Browns, the Ernie Stautners and the Gino Marchettis. What an incredible honor!

Being inducted into the Hall of Fame was beyond my wildest dreams.

Soon after my induction into the Hall, a whole new world of opportunities opened up for me. I received calls to represent prestigious organizations, to be a spokesperson for major products, and to do commercials for large corporations.

I always thought that people would forget who I was after I had quit football, but thanks to the Hall of Fame that hasn't happened.

For 14 years I lived the Texas dream of playing for the Dallas Cowboys. I retired with many wonderful memories but only one nightmare.

After my career was over, I had this recurring dream at least once a year. I was standing on the sideline in uniform with gray hair sticking out from under my helmet. Coach Landry motioned to me and said, "Come here, Bob. We've got to have you in the game."

Fearing what would happen next, I responded with, "Coach, look at 'em! Look at those guys, they are so young and so big. They're going to kill me!"

He said, "Aw, no they won't. They're not going to hurt you. You get on in there. You'll be just fine."

And just as I would start jogging out onto the field, I would wake up drenched in a cold sweat.

Thank goodness it's only a dream.

25

The Camera's Eye

IN 1982 I SOLD MY DISTRIBUTORSHIP and began my new career in landscape photography. But this isn't where my interest in photography began. To tell you that story, I have to go back to 1960 and the *Ed Sullivan Show*.

In my senior year at Texas Christian University, I was selected to the country's Kodak Coaches' All-American Team that was sponsored by Eastman Kodak. We were flown to New York City and invited to appear on the *Ed Sullivan Show*. Besides the dinners and parties, we were each given a 35mm camera plus a year's supply of film. It was the first camera I ever owned, and I was fascinated with it. The camera was operated by a wind-up motor and took about 12 shots.

Over the years, I shot thousands of candid photos of the players and coaches.

After signing my contract with the Cowboys, I had enough money to buy more cameras and equipment. I immediately began taking photographs of people and places that I had encountered during my NFL career. My first subjects, of course, were the Dallas Cowboys. Over the years, I shot thousands of candid photos of the players and coaches.

At first I took shots only of my teammates, but as my skills developed, I became a photographer for the children of the players. Many of the guys have told me that if it weren't for my love of photography, they wouldn't have any photos of their kids.

Most of the guys enjoyed being photographed, but there were two players who made it very clear that they did not want their image reproduced in any way, shape, or form. Those two were Pat Toomay and Duane Thomas. Coach Landry wasn't always aware that I had my camera focused on him—especially during team meetings. If he had, he might have cut me.

Most of the guys enjoyed being photographed, but there were two players who made it very clear that they did not want their image reproduced.

In 1983 I coauthored a book entitled *Reflections* with sportswriter Sam Blair. The book is compiled from the many photos that I took during my career with Dallas. I was able to capture Cowboys history as it was being made, and every picture told a story.

While traveling with the team, I took my camera with me wherever I went. I loved photographing the old sports stadiums and really began to appreciate architectural elements and the fascinating ways that light and shadow performed across them. I began to notice the more abstract effects of composition and the unique angles of certain structures.

About this time I began to develop an interest in photography that was reminiscent of the past. I enjoyed photographing scenes of old railway yards, boarded-up fueling stations, and old paint-chipped barns and churches from bygone eras.

After I retired, my interests in photographic subjects changed once again. I truly enjoyed shooting natural settings—especially those cast in the light of a sunrise or sunset.

When I was a teenager, my family used to take fishing trips to Pagosa Springs and Durango, Colorado. It was such a beautiful area that I came back to photograph the mountains of the region. Some of my photos include an old deserted mine shaft, covered with snow, sitting alongside a beautiful stream.

The rural areas of Throckmorton, Texas, brought back many of my childhood memories—memories of windmills gently nestled in a sea of golden grass, turning softly as warm, mild breezes gently glided through their sails. I was quickly drawn to these types of images and was fortunate enough to capture them on film.

Of all the photographs I have taken, my favorite subjects are those of deserts and canyons. Some of greatest photographic challenges have been the red rocks of the Four Corners region and the towering buttes of Utah. Natural lighting and atmospheric conditions play an exceptional role in the outcome of the perfect shot. Sometimes I would wait hours, days, or longer for the perfect lighting and conditions.

Natural lighting and atmospheric conditions play an exceptional role in the outcome of the perfect shot.

There is one photo in particular that I have entitled *Monument Valley Moonrise*. This photo displays a rare phenomenon—the illumination of all three buttes beneath a full moon. I continued to return to Monument Valley for four years in order to finally capture this extraordinary image.

The same type of patience and skill was required when I shot the Slot Canyon photographs in Paige, Arizona. The condition of light that was needed to capture this scene was available only four months out of the year, and even then there were only a few hours or possibly minutes of any given day that the image could be captured.

In June 2004 I was featured as a cover story in *Petersen's Photographic Magazine*. Several of my images were included in the story.

Appendix:
Stats, Accolades, Honors,
and Achievements

Robert Lewis Lilly

- Enshrined into the Pro Football Hall of Fame—1980

- Defensive Tackle—6′5″ 260 pounds

- High School: Throckmorton, Texas, and Pendleton, Oregon

- Texas Christian University

- NFL Draft: 1961, Round 1, Pick 13

- 1961–1974 Dallas Cowboys

- Born July 26, 1939, in Olney, Texas

- Cowboys' first-ever draft choice (1961), first Hall of Fame member (1980). Foundation of Dallas's Doomsday Defense. Had unusual speed, strength, intelligence, and recovery ability. All-NFL/NFC eight years. Played in five NFL/NFC title games and two Super Bowls. Missed just one game in 14 years.

Pro Career Highlights

- Pro Bowls—11

- NFL 75th Anniversary Team, All-Time Team, NFL 1960s All-Decade Team, NFL 1970s All-Decade Team, Dallas Cowboys Ring of Honor, Pro Football Hall of Fame (1980), College Football Hall of Fame (1981)

College Career Highlights

- Two-time All–Southwest Conference pick and a Consensus All-American at Texas Christian University; 2006 inductee to the East-West Shrine Game Hall of Fame

Additional Notes

- First draft pick in Cowboys franchise history. Missed just one NFL game during his 14-year career. Has attended the induction of each Ring of Honor inductee. First player who spent his entire career with the Cowboys to be elected to the Pro Football Hall of Fame. Starred in a number of television commercials for hardware stores and products.

Sources

Adler, James. "Super Bowl V." http://football.about.com/cs/superbowl/a/bl_superbowl5.htm (accessed December 9, 2007).

Bendetson, William. "Bob Lilly: A Photo Finish." http://proxy.espn.go.com/nfl/news/story?id=2912728 (accessed June 23, 2007).

Bob Lilly's official website, http://www.boblilly.com.

Brown, Chip. "Leading the troops; grand finale: UT's '48 bowl win capped a solid career," *Dallas Morning News,* February 2000 (special edition about Tom Landry 1924–2000).

Carroll, Bob, Michael Gershman, David Neft, and John Thorn. *Total Football II: The Official Encyclopedia of the National Football League.* New York: HarperCollins, 1997.

Carter, Al. "On a mission: Small-town values shaped big winner in Mission, Texas." *Dallas Morning News,* February 2000 (special edition about Tom Landry 1924–2000).

Cohen, Mark (TCU Athletics Media Relations Director). Texas Christian University's 1957–1960 *Football Media Guides.*

Crevier, Scott. "1967 NFL Championship: The Ice Bowl; Sunday, December 31, 1967, at Lambeau Field." The South End Zone, http://www.southendzone.com/packer.g/1967 (accessed October 17, 2007).

DallasCowboys.com. "Super Bowl VI." http://www.dallascowboys.com/history_superBowl.cfm?sb=6.

Garrison, Walt, and Mark Stallard. *Then Landry Said to Staubach...: The Best Dallas Cowboys Stories Ever Told.* Chicago: Triumph Books, 2007.

Golenbock, Peter. *Cowboys Have Always Been My Heroes: The Definitive Oral History of America's Team.* New York: Warner Books, 1997.

Golenbock, Peter. *Landry's Boys: An Oral History of a Team and an Era.* Chicago: Triumph Books, 2005.

Gosselin, Rick. "The great innovator: Hall of famer Landry originated flex defense, shotgun." *Dallas Morning News,* February 2000 (special edition about Tom Landry 1924–2000).

Harris, Cliff, and Charlie Waters. *Tales from the Dallas Cowboys: A Collection of the Greatest Stories Ever Told.* Champaign, IL: Sports Publishing LLC, 2003.

Landry, Tom, and Gregg Lewis. *Tom Landry: An Autobiography.* New York: HarperCollins, 1990.

Lilly, Bob, and Sam Blair. *Reflections: The Birth of America's Team As Seen Through the Camera of the Dallas Cowboys' First Hall of Fame Player.* Dallas, TX: Taylor Publishing Company, 1983, 1992.

Maraniss, David. *When Pride Still Mattered: A Life of Vince Lombardi.* New York: Simon and Schuster, 2005.

Monk, Cody. *Legends of the Dallas Cowboys.* Champaign, IL: Sports Publishing LLC, 2004.

Moore, David. "Building America's Team: Cowboys' architect laid foundation on faith, leadership." *Dallas Morning News,* February 2000 (special edition about Tom Landry 1924–2000).

National Football League. "The Colts get revenge: January 17, 1971." http://www.supernfl.com/SuperBowl/sb5.html (accessed January 12, 2008).

Pro Football Reference, www.pro-football-reference.com (accessed February 18, 2008).

Rentzel, Lance. *When All the Laughter Died in Sorrow.* New York: Saturday Review Press, 1972.

Sabol, Steve. *NFL Films Presents: Bob Lilly.* NFL Films. November 2005.

Sham, Brad. *Stadium Stories, Dallas Cowboys: Colorful Tales of America's Team.* Guilford, CT: Globe Pequot Press, 2003.

St. John, Bob. "Redbirds chirp bye-bye, Cowboys." *Dallas Morning News,* November 17, 1970.

Stein, Marc. "Giant start: Player-coach began his legacy in New York." *Dallas Morning News,* February 2000 (special edition about Tom Landry 1924–2000).

Taylor, Jean-Jacques. "Following the leader: Five disciples made their own way as NFL head men." *Dallas Morning News,* February 2000 (special edition about Tom Landry 1924–2000).

About the Authors

Bob Lilly

Bob Lilly graduated from Texas Christian University—which he attended on a football scholarship—with All-American honors in 1961. Upon graduating, Lilly became the first draft choice of the new Dallas Cowboys football team. During his 14-year career with the Cowboys, he was named All-Pro seven times and played in 11 All-Star games. When he retired in 1975, the Cowboys honored him by inscribing his name into Texas Stadium's Ring of Honor. In 1980 Bob was the first Dallas Cowboy enshrined in the Pro Football Hall of Fame in Canton, Ohio, and in 1981 he was inducted into the College Football Hall of Fame. The Pro Football Hall of Fame selection committee honored Bob again in August 2000 when they elected him to the NFL All-Time Team.

After his retirement from football, Lilly successfully operated a beverage-distribution business for eight years. In 1984 he moved to Las Cruces, New Mexico, where he began his career as a landscape photographer and operated his own photo gallery.

He continues to enjoy and expand his repertoire of photographic artwork.

In 1997 Bob moved to Sun City, Texas, where he and his wife, Ann, enjoy having their four married children and twelve grand-children, all of whom live in Texas, come to visit.

Kristine Setting Clark

University of San Francisco graduate and author Dr. Kristine Setting Clark is a feature writer for the San Francisco 49ers' *Gameday* magazine. She has authored three other books: *Undefeated, Untied, and Uninvited*, about the 1951 University of San Francisco Dons foot-ball team's solidarity in response to prejudice in American sports; *St Clair: I'll Take It Raw*, an exclusive, autho-rized biography of former San Francisco 49er and Hall of Fame member Bob St. Clair; and *Legends of the Hall: 1950s*, a detailed look at Pro Football Hall of Fame members from the golden era when men were men and the grass was still real.

In 1977 Kristine was diagnosed with Stage IV Hodgkin's Disease and was given three months to live. She eventually beat the dis-ease after enduring 10 months of blindness caused by the gruel-ing chemotherapy treatments. She is in the process of writing her memoir, *Don't Call Me Courageous!*, and the television treatment has been written by Jamie Williams, former San Francisco 49er tight end and screenwriter of the movie *Any Given Sunday*.

Dr. Clark resides in Northern California with her husband and has two grown children and a grandson. Her grandson, Justin, is Hall of Fame member Bob St. Clair's godson.